THINK OUT OF THE BOX

Generate Ideas on Demand, Improve Problem Solving, Make Better Decisions, and Start Thinking Your Way to the Top

Som Bathla

www.sombathla.com

Your Free Gift

As a token of my thanks for taking out time to read my book, I would like to offer you a free gift:

Click Below and Download your **Free PDF ebook.**

Learn 5 Mental Shifts To Turbo-Charge Your Performance In Every Area Of Your Life - in Next 30 Days!

You can also grab your FREE GIFT by typing in the below URL:

https://sombathla.lpages.co/5mentalshifts_totb/

Table of Contents

Chapter 1: Introduction 6

An Out of the Box Story 6

Real-world Out of the Box Examples 11

What This Book Can Do For You? 16

Chapter 2: Brain Anatomy - Where Creativity Lives..20

Why Your Brain is Like a Box? 20

Where did "Think Out of the Box" come from?..23

Let's Peep Inside the Brain............................27

Chapter 3: Building Inner Infrastructure for Out-of the Box Thinking 35

Why Belief is Everything.................................35

3 Key Challenges in Building Creativity Beliefs 40

Techniques to Instill Creativity Beliefs....43

How to Put Everything together to Think out of the Box. 55

Chapter 4: Preset Challenge and Install Routines to Start Thinking Differently.........59

Set Challenge to Prompt Out of The Box Thinking. 60

Daily Routines To Nurture Creativity Day After Day 67

Chapter 5: Effective Techniques to Think Out of Box 80

Feed Your Mind Immensely 80

Idea Fusion to Generate Idea Babies 87

Do SCAMPER to get Loads of Ideas Instantly 93

How Multi-tasking This Way Improves Creativity 99

Become an Idea Machine- Set up Daily Idea Quota 106

Embrace Boredom to Let Ideas Emerge 108

Chapter 6: Effective Strategies to Think Out of Box –continued 117

Doubt Every Default or Assumption 117

Questions. Questions. Questions = Ideas. Ideas and Ideas 120

Talk to Non-Experts For Great Ideas 125

How to use Procrastination to incubate Ideas 128

Just Chill Technique 134

Conclusion..141

May I ask you for a small favor? 143

Full Book Summary..145

Preview of the book "Make Smart Choices"
....157

Other Books in Power-Up Your Brain Series
....165

Chapter 1: Introduction

****

"Instead of thinking outside the box, get rid of the box."

— Deepak Chopra

An Out of the Box Story

Once, there was a poor farmer who lived with his daughter in a village. He owed a huge debt to the village head. He was working hard to earn and repay his debt by way of smaller installments every month. But despite that, the debt amount was getting bigger and bigger instead of being reduced, as the rate of interest charged by the village head was exorbitantly high.

This village head was not only greedy, but he had evil intentions. He wanted to marry the farmer's beautiful daughter, who was less than half of his age. He also knew that the burgeoning amount of loan had already put the farmer in a state of anxiety and depression, as the farmer was not only worried about putting food on the table daily, his topmost concern was his daughter's marriage and to provide for her better future.

Knowing all that, the village head thought of exploiting the farmer's unfortunate situation and proposed him with an offer that could alleviate all the problems of the farmer once and for all. He offered to forego the farmer's entire debt and interest, if his daughter would agree to play one game. In the game, there was a non-transparent steel jar that would contain two pebbles in it – one black and the other white. The farmer's daughter just needed to put her hand in the jar with closed eyes and pick out one of the pebbles from a jar without looking inside.

Here were the conditions of the game:

   a. If she picked a black pebble, the debt would be forgiven.
   b. However, if she picks a white pebble, the debt would still be forgiven but she had to marry that village head.

The farmer was hesitant and skeptical of the intentions of the village head, as he didn't want to put her daughter's life in jeopardy by letting her marry the wicked village head. But his daughter somehow convinced him to play the game, as she wanted to sincerely help her father get rid of all his financial woes. Moreover, there was still a 50% chance for her to win, i.e. waiver of the loan without marrying the village head.

Next day, the farmer, his daughter, the village head, and some other villagers went to gravel (a piece of land covered with pebbles). A random villager was asked to quickly pick two pebbles (one black, one white) and put them in the jar.

But as you might have guessed, how could the village head, being so greedy and wicked, have such a big offer to waive the loan solely on 50% probability and lose his money without getting married to the farmer's daughter. In fact, the evil village head had already bribed that stranger to somehow secretly ensure that he put both white pebbles in the jar. However, since her entire life was on stake, while nobody else could notice, the farmer's daughter observed this mischief.

Now for a moment, assume you are there in her situation. What will you do?

There seem to be only two options:

Alternative 1: Don't say anything, pick up one of the white pebbles, lose the game, and marry the evil guy.

Alternative 2: Publicly reveal that the jar has two white pebbles.

She obviously didn't want to marry him, so option 1 was not the preferred choice. But she wanted to definitely help her father by getting his loan forgiven so that both she and her father could lead a better life. But she also knew that if she opted for option 2, then the village head would get annoyed and make their life more miserable.

She was in a fix, but then she thought for a moment and went ahead.

Following the rules of the game, she picked up one pebble from the jar. But before showing it to anyone she dropped it in the gravel in a way that it seemed like a mistake. Fortunately, since the gravel was all covered with mixed white and black pebbles, no one could tell which one she picked.

She apologized for her mistake, but smartly suggested that if some villagers could check the other pebble remaining in the jar, it could then be determined easily which pebble she had picked. There was no reason to disagree with the daughter's suggestion, so the village head had to agree.

It seemed so natural to everyone when the villager picked out a white pebble from the jar. Therefore it meant that the girl had picked the black pebble.

Therefore, following the rules of the game, picking up black pebble entitled the girl to get the loan of her father waived without getting married to the village head. The village head guy was bewildered and got frustrated but couldn't say anything because she won fair and square, as it appeared on the face of it.

Here the girl played the smart game secretly out-of-the-jar by following the out-of the-box thinking approach.

You see how the girl created a third option, while there were seemingly only two options.

For a moment, assume even if she had called out that the game was unfair, the stranger could have said he did it by mistake, and he would pick two pebbles again and put them in the jar. But even in that option she would still run a 50% chance of losing. The option she took was not obvious to anyone but it guaranteed her win by taking advantage of the rigged game. By out of the box thinking, she created 100% secure option that made her help her father as well as safeguard herself from getting into the trap of the evil village head.

I read this story somewhere. I'm not sure if this is true or merely a work of fiction, but obviously it isn't so imaginative and unreal like the time travel scenes you see in the sci-fi movies. Regardless of the fact of whether the story was fictional or true instance, there is a real message that resonates 100% when it comes to looking at the different alternatives in our lives.

Do we only look at the limited visible options for solving any problem or do we use our brain to generate some novel and unique thoughts that open up newer and unforeseen alternatives, which can put us on the faster track to solve our problems in a better manner?

In most of the cases, we don't go beyond what is obvious and therefore limit ourselves to only those available options that everyone else sees. Consequently, such option is bound to give mediocre results, as everybody would follow suit.

For a moment, imagine how your life would be, if you could generate thoughts and ideas that others are not able to see. Wouldn't it transform the way you make choices and thus get better results?

Obviously, this would immensely improve your confidence and thus the quality of your life.

Before we move ahead, let's get some more flavor of how thinking out of the box operates by looking at some real-world examples, where out of the box thinking approach transformed many businesses.

Real-world Out of the Box Examples
For the first example, let me ask you what comes to your mind instantly when you hear the name, Philips.

Even today, for most people, Philips is a brand name that is synonymous with electronic equipment like television, music or sound system and related stuff. Of course, Philips started with electronics, but today, the majority percentage of revenue of Philips is contributed by an altogether different product line i.e. healthcare products.

Currently, healthcare products are the major contributors to the top line and the bottom line of Philips. Some might wonder how an electronic home appliance company ventured out in a totally different industry of manufacturing medical equipment and garnered so much profitability that it exceeded the sales and profits of its initial product line, i.e., electronics?

It definitely was out of the box thinking approach to transition from one product model to an entirely different range of unrelated product segment. Producing a microwave oven versus producing an incubator for a new born baby although both of them are machines, but till the time Philips thought within the box of home appliances, no one could think of getting into healthcare products.

It was only when they realized that the technology used in manufacturing home appliance could be applied to producing healthcare products by meeting certain different specifications. It was this out of the box thinking that made them transition into an entirely new business vertical.

Let's take another example.

BIC, a French company initially started with all kinds of writing products, i.e., pencils and other stationery products like ballpoint pens, markers, colors etc. But later on, they shifted from paper products to other unrelated products vis-à-vis stationery items. They started producing razors, lighters, perfumes, etc.

What made them expand to another unrelated type of product line?

In fact, they thought of their existing business in an altogether different way. While they initially believed that their business was just about creating writing products, here, the company adopted an out of the box thinking approach. They realized that their business could be categorized as a business of manufacturing disposable items. Once they thought about their business from this new lens, anything that could be disposed of became their business model, hence manufacturing lighters, razors, perfumes etc. was not something that they could ignore further.

What it took was thinking out of the box from "writing products" to "disposable products." And that made them expand in different verticals.

Let's take one example from the world of sports. For a moment, if you think of athletes before Roger Bannister, a British athlete, they never thought that running one mile in less than 4 minutes was even humanly possible. Even the coaches of Roger Bannister mocked him off at first when Roger apprised them about him taking a challenge of running a mile in less than 4 minutes. But on May 6, 1954, Roger Bannister with unconventional thinking clubbed with dedication and commitment proved that the old belief about human impossibility of running a mile in less than 4 minutes was a limited in-the-box-thinking approach only.

Today, you see out of the box thinking happening all around at such a rapid pace leading to massive technological development and innovation. If you look around, you'll see so many creative ideas taking shape that just two generations ago would have appeared like some hypothetical science fiction story.

Imagine the pace of evolution of humans from the time when people used to think that the earth was at the center of the universe (and the sun was rotating around the earth in orbits) to a realization, where we are thinking not only about space travel, but also developing space tourism– thanks to out of the box thinkers like Elon Musk and Richard Branson. Hundreds of people including Ashton Kutcher, Leonardo DiCaprio, and Justin Bieber already placed a deposit for space travel for USD 250,000 for *Unity* Spacecraft, a Richard Branson's space travel initiative.

Today, a small robot (with artificial intelligence) can do so many tasks for you from selecting music, switching our lights on or off or making calls for you – think about Alexa (from Amazon).

What do all these stories talk about?

They only exemplify the role of creative or innovating thinking or what we often term as thinking out of the box and how it has transformed human experience so far and will continue to do so.

What This Book Can Do For You?
Of course, we can go on and on with so many real-life stories of innovation and out of box thinking that this book can be titled "Thinking out of the Box Stories."

But I know that you don't want only that. You want to know how you can get started with out of the box thinking in your life, to solve your problems and achieve your goals. You want to know how you can develop your cognitive abilities, so you could generate more creative ideas and gain an edge over others in terms of providing solutions.

This book will change how you perceive your creativity, while stripping creativity itself of its mystique. If you are able to generate ideas that deliver results, it has the potential to shift the trajectory of your life.

You will perhaps start seeing endless possibilities stretching before you. You will learn how to:

- Generate ideas on demand.
- Find new ways to make money.
- Create new business opportunities.
- Manipulate and modify existing ideas to make them powerful.
- Create new products, services, and processes.
- Develop solutions to complex business problems.

- See problems as opportunities.
- Become more productive.
- Be the "idea person" in your organization.
- Know where to look for the "breakthrough idea."

Above is just to list a few benefits.

I want to equip you with the most effective strategies that will help you think out of the box and help you get creative ideas on demand. I know it's a big promise, but here is the thing. The strategies I'm telling in the book are not something invented by me, rather they are used by the many creative thinkers of the world. Since they have worked for them, it should work for you and me as well (yes, I'm on the same journey).

Out of the Box Thinking is for anyone and everyone.

Don't think that generating creative ideas is something that is reserved only for some artistic personalities like painters, writers, musicians, or some other creative tribe. Also, don't misunderstand that out-of-the-box thinking is only for superbly talented entrepreneurs who want to put a dent in the world.

Don't set yourself into some secluded category and limit yourself for a conventional path that delivers just mediocre results. Creative thinking is for anyone who wants to think and act differently from the standard way of doing things. Thinking of different ways of arriving at best solutions by spending lesser time, money, and energy is and should be the objective of every growth-oriented individual.

Therefore, with that, let's start diving deeper to understand the concept better in the next chapter before you learn the practical ways to think out-of-the-box in the later sections of the book.

Introduction: Key Takeaways

Even if you apparently find limited alternatives to any problem, there are still more solutions to any problem; and that's possible with out of the box thinking.

Individuals and organizations equally can challenge their existing way of operations and observe the things by shifting their perspective and approach of looking at any problem. The personal, as well as organization level examples, demonstrate that out of the box thinking opens up new paradigms and widens the perspective of looking at the world.

Also, **out of box thinking is not uniquely gifted to some artistic profile people, nor**

is it limited to reality-bending world-changing successful entrepreneurs. Anyone can develop their creative thinking faculties and generate surprisingly new and unpredictable ways of solving problems, if they believe so and are willing to spend time and effort in learning how to do think out of the box.

This book is a roadmap to **learning and implementing the strategies for every growth oriented individual** who want to explore and lead their life in a way that they couldn't have comprehended earlier.

Chapter 2: Brain Anatomy - Where Creativity Lives

****

"When the brain is whole, the unified consciousness of the left and right hemispheres adds up to more than the individual properties of the separate hemispheres."

~ Roger Sperry

Why Your Brain is Like a Box?

Imagine what comes to your mind when you hear the word "Out of the Box." You'll immediately visualize an image of the box that's open.

The next thing you'll try to see is what's inside the box and what's outside.

When you imagine looking inside the box, you'll have these two instant observations:

Quantity: The box has four walls and closed sides from the top and bottom; therefore, only certain limited quantity of things can be accommodated inside the box. For example, you can't store 100 packages in a box, when it has the storage capacity for only 40 items. Inside the box, there is a *limitation of the quantity* that can be stored.

Type of Contents: Also depending on the size of the items you put in the box, there will be uniformity of the type of the contents of the box with a little variation.

Take an example, if some box is designed to store and take the weight of certain specific number cookies packets, you won't risk storing heavyweight steel items inside the box, because you know that the box won't sustain the heavy weight. Therefore, inside the box, there is a *limitation of the types of contents* as well.

Unfortunately, most people use their brain like boxes. Let's try to understand this better.

The box of our mind is designed by involuntary influences (almost most of the times) of our parents, teachers, immediate friend circle, the society we live in or the religion we follow, since our childhood till we start to live independently financially.

We mistakenly think we have control over the decisions we make. But unfortunately our "so-called" conscious decisions are often misguided by the involuntary imprints of our surrounding environments. Most of the decisions we make for our every day matters, as well as important life decisions, are strongly affected by the ingrained belief system due to years or decades of social conditioning.

And sadly, this becomes a preset pattern for most of us, unless someone chooses to heighten their level of consciousness by exposing themselves to a different environment and choose to think beyond the influence of conditioned thinking. Therefore, the quality, as well as the quantity of content in our mind (i.e., our thoughts and creativity), becomes limited only to the extent of the design (conditioning) of our mind's box.

If you ask a frog who has always lived its entire life in a well about what it thinks about the world, it will make a jump from one side of the well to another, and happily explain that this is the world. You realize that this is such a distorted world view. However, if you ask another frog who sees the world sitting at the beach of an ocean, its perspective of the world will be grand and limitless.

Similarly, if you are born and brought up in a family that believes in taking life as an adventure, and about experimenting, you will think life as a journey of exploration. However, if you are raised in a conservative and risk-averse family, you won't be able to think much beyond what is normal because of your upbringing, unless you consciously or somehow get exposed to an environment.

Where do you find yourself in terms of your thinking?

There is some fun exercise that has been used for many decades to see how people think, and you'll also come to know the genesis of the phrase " Think Out of the Box."

Where did "Think Out of the Box" come from?

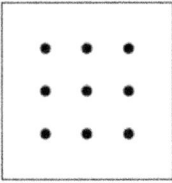

Above image shows 9 dots and below is the exercise you need to do.

You are required to combine these 9 dots in one go without lifting the pencil and without any repetition over any of the dots.

Just pause now for a minute and apply your mind to solve this puzzle. Don't read any further, unless you have given it a try to solve this.

Okay, hope you are back now after completing the exercise. You can find the right answer at the end of this chapter.

If you have tried solving this puzzle, as most people do, you might have realized that your first attempts **usually involved sketching lines inside the imaginary square.** But the answer doesn't lie inside the box. The correct solution requires you to draw lines that extend beyond the area defined by the dots- i.e., out of the imaginary square or box.

This 9-dot puzzle exemplifies the concept that thinking outside the box is to look further and to try not thinking of the obvious things but to try thinking of the things beyond them. That to find new and better solution to problems one needs to be imaginative enough to think outside the boundaries – means the ability to see beyond what's obvious.

This 9-dot puzzle originally appeared in a 1914 book written by Sam Lloyd titled the *Cyclopedia of Puzzles*. But this puzzle became popular in the 1960s and the 1970s, when the management consultants started to offer their clients a challenge to solve this to test their lateral thinking skills.

This formed the genesis of this often quoted phrase, *Think Out Of The Box,* and has since become the catchphrase or cliché and is used mostly by management consultants and executive coaches.

Majority of the people live their entire life thinking "inside the box" only – in the pre-conditioned thinking mode only. Even huge corporations at times, got in the traps of limited "inside the box" thinking and suffered adversely to the extent that they got out of the business. If you want to see the evidence in the business world of *inside the box thinking*, they are many. Let's look at a few of them and compare them with out-of-the-box thinking before we start digging deeper inside our brains

How Thinking Inside the Box kills Growth

Kodak was a successful print camera company of its time. During the later years of the twentieth century when digital photography was emerging, Kodak didn't pay the required attention to this new disruptive digital technology and all but ignored the digital wave. Despite the fact that *digital* photography was invented by a Kodak engineer, the management simply ignored his own employee's invention.

And the aftermath of such limited thinking we all know. Other aggressive companies came and took the benefit of the ride of digital cameras and in no time took substantial market share. Finally, in 2012, Kodak had to file for bankruptcy.

Take the example of another famous company Blockbuster, a DVD renting company, one of the most successful companies in the movie distribution space. But they restricted themselves to their older inside-the-box-thinking approach.

In the year 2000, CEO of Blockbuster even laughed at Netflix founders, when the latter offered a partnership to work jointly in the offline and digital world. Thinking digital in the wave of the internet was definitely an out-of-the-box thinking approach by Netflix. Failing to think out of their old patterns, Blockbuster just like Kodak had to go for bankruptcy in the year 2010. The irony is that today's generation doesn't even know if a company like Blockbuster existed. On the other hand, Netflix is ranked as one of the Fortune's top 100 fastest-growing companies.

The examples above show the entirely different approaches followed by inside-the-box thinkers and out-of-the-box thinkers.

But here is the thing.

Most people mistakenly believe that not all people are capable of thinking creatively- they think that some people have their brain designed that way that they think differently, while most people can't think beyond what they can see. But neuroscience and advancement of technology have proven that each of us is equipped with the required machinery in our brains to do out-of-box-thinking.

To understand this, let's dissect your brain and see that not merely a few people, rather everyone is equipped with infrastructure in their brains that enables each of us to think creatively and out of the box.

Let's Peep Inside the Brain
Before 1950, humanity's view was that the essential part of the brain was the left hemisphere i.e., the same side of the body that housed the heart. Around the 1800s, there was

evidence that it was only the left brain that understood the words and language that human speak. The other hemisphere of the brain, i.e., the right brain was considered to be retarded, instinctive and that it served its purpose in the primitive age, but with the technological advancements, it had outgrown its importance. And therefore, according to scientists, the left brain was considered superior.

But it was only in the 1950s, when Roger Sperry, who is famous for the split-brain research and won a Nobel Prize in medicine, discovered that the right brain is in fact the superior portion of the brain. He stated, "The so-called subordinate or minor hemisphere, which we had formerly supposed to be illiterate and mentally retarded and thought by some authorities to not even be conscious, was found to be in fact the superior cerebral member when it came to performing certain kinds of mental tasks."

Sperry further stated that the left and right hemisphere indicated two different modes of thinking. The left brain was more into reasoning things sequentially; more analysis-oriented, and handled the words. On the other hand, the right brain was more of reasoning holistically, recognizing the patterns, and interpreting the emotions and non-verbal expressions.

Sperry was awarded the Nobel Prize for this research, and this transformed the way neuroscience and psychology started to view the mind and its internal operations. When Sperry died in 1994, the New York Times quoted him as a man who "overturned the prevailing orthodoxy that the left hemisphere was the dominant part of our brains"

In the year 1979, Betty Edwards, an American art teacher and author, wrote a great book *"Drawing on the Right Side of Brain"* that dived way deeper into the concepts of how right brain thinking works. She rejected the belief that some people just aren't artistic. Her view was that drawing was not that very difficult, rather the way people see it is the problem.

Edwards' work was based in part on her understanding of neuroscience, especially the cerebral hemisphere research which suggested that the two hemispheres of the brain have different functions. But instead of focusing more on the locations of the hemispheres, she termed the modes "L-mode" and "R-mode." She described L-mode as basically a verbal, analytic, sequential mode of thinking, and R-mode as basically visual, perceptual, and global.

Not only innovation by Robert Sperry and later popularization of the concept of right-hemisphere by Betty Edwards, the technology had also been a game changer in understanding the brain better in the past few decades. The invention of fMRI (function Magnetic Resonance Imaging) enabled man to track the movement and function of neurons inside the brain through scanning and imagination. fMRI showed the evidence by showing the movement of blood to some specific portions of the brain, while performing different functions.

For example, if you are doing some complex mathematical problem, the scan would show the thick appearance of blood in the left hemisphere. On the other hand, while involving in some artistic work, watching some emotional movie, or doing some mind wandering, the portions in the right hemisphere showed more blood cells providing the required energy to the brain.

In a nutshell, towards the latter half of the 20th Century, the myth that the left hemisphere or say, the left brain was superior to the right brain was shattered. It was concluded that both portions of the brain play a significant role in discharging the different activities within the brain.

Let's understand some key differences between the left brain and the right brain:

- The left brain is analytical i.e., it goes deeper into a specific problem and finds the reasoning behind the problem; the right brain synthesizes different pieces of information and looks at the bigger picture.

- The left brain is specialized in looking at the texts and numbers; the right brain looks at the broader contexts in which the information is being presented.

- The left brain controls the right side of body; the right brain controls the left side of the body.

- The left brain looks at the things in a sequence, whereas the right brain looks at things simultaneously.

So far, we talked about the left and right brain as if they are two entirely distinct functional units and that you have to switch on or off one or the other side of the brain. But this is not the right approach. Both hemispheres can complement each other while taking decisions by looking at the macro big picture scenarios as well as micro mini-details.

While it was true that for many years, the left brain had dominated the way the world of business works. Because most of the work in the industrial age (manual work through the use of industrial machines), as well as in the information age (the knowledge work through the use of technology), required the application of logical and analytical skills of human beings, and therefore more usage of the left logical brain.

But with the consistent and fast-paced automation of knowledge work, and due to rapid progress in the field of artificial intelligence, most of the left brain capability work can be handled by machines. As reported[1], McDonald had already initiated the process of running its stores by McRobots applying the artificial intelligence that works with 50 times more speed and accuracy than humans. This is because artificial intelligence works pretty well when there is a clear process of doing things in a defined and logical way.

Now that you understand the broad mechanism about how both sides of our brain work, you also understand that you cannot thrive anymore merely by relying on the logical side of the brain and ignoring the right brain i.e., imaginative creative thinking.

Therefore, the next step is to ask how you can put this knowledge into practice.

You must be curious to know the techniques through which out-of-the-box thinking works for you. I believe that you are more interested in knowing the proven strategies and techniques that will empower you to think on your feet and generate ideas on demand.

Therefore, we will now get straight into the meat. From here onwards, we will get into the "How-to's," with specific instructions, so you can start implementing them in your everyday life.

Let's get into the next chapter where you will learn about building your inner infrastructure and a solid foundation to start thinking creatively.

Annexure: 9 Dot Problem Solution

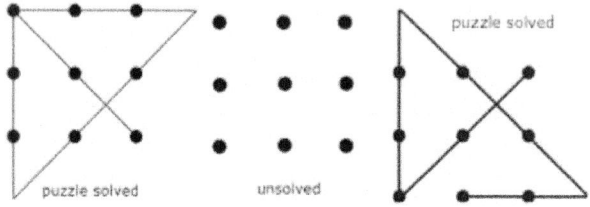

Chapter 2: Key Takeaways

Your thinking can be compared to a box. The box has limitation about storing a specific quantity, as well as only specific type of items can be put in a particular box. Similarly our minds tend to think in a particular way all the time, which is generally limited in nature and controlled by the type of thoughts that are unconsciously fed in our brains since our childhood till we become independent adults. The result is the **human mind thinks only in a certain specific conditioned way.**

The 9-dot exercise helps you assess your way of thinking, whether you follow the conventional inside the box approach or go out of the box to solve the problem innovatively. The only way to thinking differently and creatively is to come out of the limited box and experience the limitless options around you, unforeseeable from inside-the-box thinking approach.

Before science could look deeper into the brain i.e. until the middle of the twentieth century, **it was believed that the left brain is the superior portion of our brain**, and the other side i.e., the right brain is a retarded and impractical dreamer stuff, which doesn't serve any utility for the material world outside.

Thanks to the research by Robert Sperry, Nobel Prize winner, where he showed to the world **that the right hemisphere plays a very important role** by giving a bigger context and understanding of the outside world. Later Betty Edwards, through her book "Drawing from the Right Side of The Brain" and neuroscience, through the innovation of fMRI clearly confirmed how both sides of the brain work.

Each of the brain functions discharged different functions- the left brain controls the right side of the body and vice-versa. The left is sequential, the right is simultaneous. The left brain looks at the text, and the right one focuses on the context. The left brain is analytical, while the right brain synthesizes the information.

Chapter 3: Building Inner Infrastructure for Out-of the Box Thinking

****

"If I have the belief that I can do it, I shall surely acquire the capacity to do it even if I may not have it at the beginning."

~Gandhi

Why Belief is Everything

We have often heard that belief plays a vital role in achieving anything, but most people just know it on the surface level only- merely at the intellectual level, and they have not experienced the same at their deeper level of consciousness.

Then there are other sets of people, who consider themselves as more of logical and rational beings – and these sets of people find such discussions about belief a bit of mystical and wishy-washy thinking.

But here is the fact. No matter what you think, the truth is:

Belief is not merely a vital part of any major accomplishment; rather, belief is EVERYTHING before you take even the first step in any direction.

You will not commit to any action until you have a strong belief in your mind that it's possible for you. Take any example in your life. Until you believed in the possibility of any goal for you, you didn't take any action. This belief generates a deeper knowing that the goal is possible for you – it generates a sense of certainty of outcome in your mind.

Let me give you a personal example of my life. After my graduation, my father wanted me to go for management studies that required clearing the competitive entrance examination. I didn't opt for going to a highly competitive management studies entrance examination, because somehow I had a limiting belief (after hearing my surrounding environment numerous times – the negative effects of growing up in smaller town) that it would be too hard for me to surpass the initial hurdle of the entrance examination and get admission to a good management school.

I rather believed myself to be just another small-town kid, who lacked confidence in his ability for that assignment, so I couldn't even muster up the courage to attempt it.

What was the lesson for me?

Simple. No belief, no action.

On the contrary, when I had inculcated a belief in myself that I could run 10 Kilometers in one stretch or I could write books to spread my knowledge and experience to the world, I started taking actions. And the results are nothing but taking the right actions consistently. Hence, I was able to run 10 kilometers in one stretch within 8-10 weeks of right training and practice. I also plunged myself to switch my career from a corporate day job to become a full-time authorpreneur.

All this happened because I had developed a stronger belief that things are possible for me, despite the fact that I never had any serious interest in sports earlier, neither had I had any strong literary instincts to pursue content creation much later as my career.

What was different here?

Again, not something very complex. It's a simple formula.

The stronger the belief, the massive the actions, the greater the results, and this moves in a cycle. Greater results strengthen beliefs, which in turn pump you to put in more efforts.

If you don't believe (or maybe you don't' want to believe) that you can climb the Mount Everest, you won't take any action. On the other hand, there are people like Arunima Sinha, an Indian athlete who despite losing her leg in an accident believed strongly that she could climb the Everest with artificial limbs. She has now climbed all the highest peaks across all the seven continents of the world. That's the power of generating a stronger belief.

I know you might be wondering why I am talking so much about beliefs while you came here to understand how to develop your creative thinking ability.

It's for a specific reason. I urge you to look at the heading of this chapter. This chapter is all about building an inner environment for thinking out of the box and having a strong belief that you can think creatively is the underpinning before you move further on this direction.

How Just Believing Makes You More Creative

There was a study conducted in a major publishing company to find out why some people were creative and others were not. The results of the study surprised everyone because all other things being equal, there was only one factor that determined whether the person will be creative or not.

Here is what the results showed: The group who believed that they were creative, was creative and the other group of people who believed otherwise was not creative.

Seems surprisingly simple but profound, isn't it?

Let's see what happened next.

As a next step, the company organized some training for "so-called" uncreative people (who believed so) to teach them effective strategies to build their belief system. After training, the results were astonishing. All of them started giving way more creative solutions and innovative ideas than the earlier set of creative people, who already believed they were creative.

That's the power of positive belief.

Creative people don't allow negative thinking or beliefs to enter into their brains. They know that negative thinking brings stressful emotions like fear, anxiety, stress, depression, etc., and once your brain is filled with all these negative emotions, you don't really have a space to think anything other than a vicious cycle of negative thinking only.

All creative people are joyful and positive about life. They believe in the possibility of outcomes. They always look at "what is" and "what can be" instead of "what is not."

Our history is filled with creative people who did not allow negative thinking to come in the way of achieving their goals. They definitely faced more frustration and embarrassment many times for not hitting their goals, but they didn't let negative thinking overpower them.

- Can you ever imagine Thomas Edison crying in the corner of his room, when he failed the 500th time in his electric bulb experiment and giving up?

- Can you think about Albert Einstein going to some lonely secluded place throwing up all his research notes, after he felt overwhelmed and frustrated in not getting the results of his research as he wanted? Sounds funny, doesn't it?

- Do you even consider it fathomable imagining successful and highly creative entrepreneurs like Richard Branson or Elon Musk getting into depression and anxiety if any of their major projects fail miserably?

I hope you got the point. Creative people believe in themselves that they can create something and this belief keeps them engaged in their endeavors on a consistent basis.

Any journey towards success goes from inside out. Therefore, the first step is to strengthen your beliefs that anyone and everyone is capable of thinking out of the box.

3 Key Challenges in Building Creativity Beliefs

Let's admit this. Our approach to handling any situation of life becomes way more positive and upbeat when we feel confident about us and our abilities i.e., when we believe in ourselves.

Everybody wants to believe in themselves, but very few achieve this.

What comes in the way?

There are three key challenges that come in the way of developing and strengthening our belief system towards positive things. They are (1) Fear; (2) Uncertainty; and (3) Doubt, let's collectively call it FUDs, as Michael Michalko, an author and a creative thinking expert terms it.

1. **Fear**: You are fearful of failure, about other people's judgment of you, fearful of wasting your time and more. Fear shows you an imaginary future that you want to avoid at all costs, so the obvious choice is to maintain the status quo, and the result is no action, and no results, and it ironically aggravates the negative beliefs.

2. **Uncertainty**: Human mind loves security and certainty of the events playing out in our lives. They don't like the idea of being uncertain about the future, barring positive types of uncertainties that we call novelty. Any uncertainty about future security puts us into the state of anxiety, which shakes our beliefs.

3. **Doubt:** We doubt ourselves being less capable of achieving something significant. Sometimes, even after achieving a reasonable success, we still doubt our abilities and tend to undermine our efforts by giving full credit to the luck. Doubts drag us into an imposter syndrome situation, where despite attaining some level of success, we feel that we don't deserve that and become fearful that our fraud might be exposed to the world.

When we are plagued with FUDs, we suppress our thinking abilities with these negative emotions, because there is secretion of a chemical called cortisol in our brains, that is a stress chemical and associates with negative moods. This results in a non-resourceful behavior, and thus, we are unable to take any action and produce results.

Under FUD's influence there is no possibility that you can come out with new ideas. Creativity needs a space in your brain where your neurons can fire with other neurons carrying different ideas and thus, wire with each other to create different neural- pathways. But the emotions generated by these FUDs take up all the spaces, leaving no room for new ideas to emerge.

I'm not saying you should totally disregard your fears and just blindly keep moving. We should pay attention and acknowledge these FUDs. But instead of them affecting us negatively, we need to focus on taking actions which will eventually empower us to overpower these negative emotions.

Techniques to Instill Creativity Beliefs

Now you know that without belief, you can't take out a single step. You also know the challenges that come in the way of developing a stronger belief, so what should you do next?

Now you need to learn the powerful ways to develop positive beliefs.

Prescott Lecky, an American psychologist who was a pioneer in self-image psychology stated that there are **two powerful levers** for changing beliefs:

1. A **belief that we are capable of doing our part of the job**, which means that we can independently control our actions.

2. A **belief that each of us has something inside of us that makes us talented and capable** as any other person on the earth and there shouldn't be anything that belittles us as compared to the world.

Though you might find this a repetition of what I stated earlier, but this is so important to understand at deeper levels. You need to frequently expose yourself to the thoughts that you want to deeply engrain in your mind, so it becomes part of you.

Only if you believe in your capability to take action and that you are as worthy and deserving as any other successful person on this planet, then your mind believes in the possibility of the outcome. And it's only then it suggests you to take the required actions necessary to achieve your goals.

Fear, doubts, and uncertainty work entirely contrary to the above two powerful belief levers that are needed to think differently and innovatively. These FUDs and Belief Levers can't co-exist in our head, and therefore we need to take some action to replace the former with the latter.

Thankfully, Lecky realized that this was easier said than done. He was mindful that replacing the beliefs that have housed in our heads for years, and in most cases, for decades is not an easy job. Your mind will offer all kinds of logic and rationales for sticking to the older set of beliefs; therefore you have to come out with strong arguments to counter your negative beliefs, before you can replace them.

Change Your Belief with this Tick-Tock Exercise

Therefore, to replace these beliefs, Lecky devised a technique called Tick Tock Exercise, especially for innovative work.

Tick-Tock is a very powerful exercise to help you overcome your fears, doubts, and uncertainties. In Tick-Tock, you write out your fears, confront them head-on, and then substitute positive factors that will allow you to succeed. Here, you counter any kind of negative belief with counter-arguments to nullify that negative belief. Once your mind accepts those arguments, it will let you replace the older beliefs with the new set of beliefs.

Here is what you'll do. Take a plain sheet of physical paper or open up your word document and draw two columnar tables therein. On the top of left-side write "Tick," and on the right side, write the word "Tock."

1. Sit quietly and write down all your negative beliefs under "Tick."
2. After this, substitute an *objective and* positive thought in the "Tock" column opposite to each *subjective*, negative belief written in the "Tick" column.

I'll offer one example showing one negative belief in the "Tick" column and counter it objectively under "Tock" column below. You can write down as many Ticks and counter them to kill those negative beliefs.

Let's take a simple example. Assume you want to start a new product in the market, which can solve some specific problems in your locality and in turn offer you good financial rewards.

Immediately with this thought, there will be a flood of thoughts in your head about why it's not possible i.e., negative thinking overpowers you. Let's understand how the negative beliefs could be replaced by using Tick Tock Exercise.

Tick (State Your Negative 'subjective' beliefs)	**Tock (State a Strong 'objective' counter-argument)**
My idea is unique but I'm not sure if the timing is right to implement this idea. I might waste time putting efforts in this idea, and even lose money in the process.	I came to this idea after I put endless hours in researching about the viability and market, and like any other new idea, no one can guarantee its success before launching, and therefore I should first put this out to the world and see how it goes.
Also, who will give me funding to back up this idea, as I don't have a success track	Why am I considering only the downsides of failure and wasting time and money? There could

record to demonstrate that I can make this product a success?	be a brighter side. Since I'm prepared enough, if I give my best shot, I can succeed with this new product. Even if it doesn't succeed, it helps me learn the ropes and I'll put it better next time. I should understand that only if I believe that my product can help others, then only I can convince others with conviction about the success. It is only my confidence and commitment to my product that will convince the investor to back up my project with the required funding.

Once you give stronger and objective counter-arguments in writing, your mind will start to validate your arguments. The older beliefs start to lose their stronghold, as you see the things from a positive outlook and perspective.

You would realize that the above hypothetical example has the potential to see things from two different perspectives. You'll be amazed to realize that your same mind that thinks negatively can generate so many positive thoughts.

Now, it's time for you to do this exercise about all your negative beliefs regarding not being able to generate better alternatives for your life problems.

Think about all your negative beliefs that you have been slowly nurturing by giving them enough time and space, that they have made a life-long nest in your head. This could be writing a bestselling book or poetry, or recording a music album someday, or it could be starting your new venture, or running a marathon, or setting up an NGO for helping your community. It could be anything that matters most to you, but your fears, uncertainty and doubts are keeping you from taking any action on them.

Take up few "TICKs," and counter them with strong "TOCKs," only to gain an insightful Tick-Tock experience that will give a shift to your mind, and soon you will start developing a new set of beliefs.

Surround Yourself with People Who Believe in You.

If you have watched the movie, *Matrix,* you can relate to this example. How the character, Morpheus (played by Laurence Fishburne), kept telling the character, Neo (played by Keanu Reeves), that he was "the one" despite Neo doubting his abilities to crack the code of Matrix. But Morpheus placed so much trust in Neo that ultimately, Neo started to believe that he was indeed the one that he gained the full access to his potential.

That's the magic of someone believing in you, as it gives you consistent reinforcement of your abilities.

In fact, there is no dearth of potential in any human being; rather, these are the fears and doubts that cripple us. Therefore, you should make friends with folks who believe in creating and designing their life. Their company will elevate you. You'll get the shoulder-rubbing effect by spending some time with them. These persons can be your friends, mentors, or coaches, who believe in you and your abilities to achieve things in life. If they are coaches, they are invested in your success because it's your results only that will prove their mettle.

Don't spend time with people who don't trust you. They create an environment of fear and negativity around you. If that person happens to be your spouse or close relative, then don't try to prove your beliefs to them, rather avoid getting into any set of arguments with them.

You must be careful enough in trying to inspire other people only to the extent that it doesn't start negatively influencing you.

Just like Tick-Tock Exercise, where you yourself offered "Tocks," i.e., objective counter-response to "Ticks," i.e., negative beliefs, staying with growth-oriented positive people will add more weight to your efforts in eradicating negative beliefs and replacing them with positive beliefs about thinking more creatively.

Self Affirmation

There is a wonderful approach that can help you imbibe any belief on autopilot basis in your head. I'm talking about self-affirmation of the beliefs by repetition until the new beliefs become part of your identity.

Let's try to understand this by way of some metaphor. Before the internet took over the whole world by storm in a span of last few years, we used to have audio cassettes and tapes to listen to music or any other audio stuff, followed by the invention of audio CDs.

One thing with audio cassettes- tapes or CDs is that you can overwrite them with new songs or audio, which means that the older songs in that tape or CD don't exist anymore, rather a new set of songs that are overwritten get stored, and we can enjoy the new songs with this simple re-recording.

Same is the case with our minds. When we are born, we really don't know any religion, faith, jurisdiction, or cultural beliefs. In other words, our mind was a blank tape or CD. Then as we grew up, we started getting imprints of thoughts and beliefs from our parents, friends, society, and culture. That means we have filled the blank audio tapes of our minds with the society's thoughts, belief, and patterns. Our mind would only play the songs that others recorded in our blank CD or audiotape.

Now add one more instance in the above example. Assume you fall in love and get married to someone who is from a different religion or faith. And since he or she is your partner, you started following some rituals or imbibing some practices of that faith in your life. Instead of going to church, you now accompany your partner to temple or other places of worship where he or she follows the rituals. This is a small bit of overwriting or rerecording of new beliefs over the past recording of beliefs.

But here is the thing.

Why allow imprints to happen only by accidents, why not selectively imprint those beliefs in our mind that are going to serve us by achieving our significant goals and ambitions?

Why don't we intentionally choose to create some new neural-pathways or patterns in our mind that make us capable of thinking and believing differently about us?

How is that possible?

It's through the power of self-affirmation.

Before we continue, let's admit that there is some wrong connotation associated with affirmations. Some people say affirmations don't work, rather they believe it's just getting swayed by some wishy-washy and mystical state, and far away from being practical or realistic. Let me admit, I was also skeptical about the effectiveness of the affirmations. It felt like making a fool of my mind with some false statements that I'm repeating blindly, which is not true, rather bluntly opposite to my reality.

But it was until I realized that the problem was not with affirmations, that the problem was with the way the affirmations are crafted.

Most self-help gurus will teach you to state affirmations in the present tense, as if you have achieved the success. Like "I'm enjoying the life like a millionaire," while in reality you are just slogging through a low-paying unsatisfying job, or "I'm in the best relationship with my spouse and kids," and the reality is something entirely opposite.

There are many problems with this kind of affirmation.

Firstly, since they don't feel real, you don't believe them. Secondly, they make you feel as if you don't need to do anything and just give you momentary pleasure until you encounter the real world. Thirdly, they aggravate the level of inner conflict between your current reality and the future goals to be attained.

There is a better way of affirmation through different kind of affirmation statements that I learned from Hal Elrod while reading his bestselling book, Miracle Morning, many years ago.

Hal says that instead of telling your mind statements that appear to be false on the face of it and feel like cheating yourself, you should use the affirmation statements that appear logical and instead, push you forward to take action.

The statement like, "I'm committed to reducing my weight by 20 pounds within 3 months, and therefore, I'm committed to taking all the necessary action including work out, diet etc, that will bring me closer to my ultimate goal" is much better than saying "I'm already thin and fit currently."

You can design your affirmation statement related to generating innovating thinking abilities by crafting something like, "I'm committed to believing in my creative abilities and generate and write 5 new ideas every day that are related to my most important projects."

Think more of your past successes than your failures

Another important strategy that can help you design your inner environment to combat the negative feelings of distrust is to be selective in what you remember about your past.

Whenever you think about the past, always focus more on the success you achieved instead of the events when you failed.

The benefit of directing your thinking towards successful memories is that you recall your traits and qualities as well as your behaviors and actions that led to the success in the past. In reality, those personal traits and those actions that enabled you to succeed in the past would need to be replicated in cementing your beliefs about you and your abilities for all your future endeavors. They will solidify your self-image as a person who can achieve any goal.

Thinking about past failures, without any intention of learning from mistakes, and just reminiscing about bad experiences, destroys your self-esteem and courage to take action on future goals.

Therefore, if you want to improve your ability to think out of the box and come out with innovative ideas and solutions, think about a time in your life when you suddenly came out with an idea, while others continued to struggle with the similar problem. It could be your school or college time, or your work related or personal family experience or anything, when you found yourself creative.

Some people might think they never had that kind of lightening idea spark in their mind ever, but that's not true. Each of us has at least a few experiences where we gave some ideas in the group, which was appreciated by others. It could even be suggesting some good family trip idea with saving or could be suggesting some approach at your work that had saved your company significant efforts or financially.

Pause reading for a moment and close your eyes to think about any such instance, and I believe that you should recall at least a few such experiences.

The more you try to recall successful events of your past, the more you give the right signals to your mind about your ability to do similar things again in the present and future.

How to Put Everything together to Think out of the Box.

According to some internet researches there are some rough estimates that a human mind generally thinks about 50,000 to 60,000 thoughts in a single day. But it becomes interesting here to note that more than 95% of those thoughts are of recurring nature.

Now, this is really bad, if you are repeating thoughts that are non-resourceful. Wherever we are in our lives currently is nothing but the results of our pre-programmed thinking only because our actions can never go beyond what we consistently think of. Buddha said that we become what we consistently think of.

Our involuntary thought process runs on its own on an autopilot basis. Ironically, the common thinking pattern of the mind is to think more of negative future outcomes, because its job is to keep you surviving and therefore it wants you to not think of anything uncomfortable or outside of your routine.

The longer you have run this old programming in your head by repetition of thoughts, the more difficult it is to reprogram coding of your software program (unless you are deeply committed to change it). However, if you consciously and voluntarily choose resourceful thoughts and affirm them loudly or subtly in your mind again and again, you will initiate the reprogramming of your mind.

In order to think creatively, you have to reprogram your old non-supportive beliefs that have convinced you that creative thinking is only for others and you're not cut out to think multiple solutions to any problem.

If you design your affirmation like, "I'm committed to deepening my faith that I can think creatively most of the time and will take all the steps that deepen my faith about thinking abilities." That's believable about a better future, and will prompt you to commit towards doing whatever it takes to develop creative ideas.

Go out of your house and find some community where you can find people who are way ahead on the same path as you want to tread and try to connect with them, or find some people virtually and connect with them.

Chapter 3 Key Takeaways

Everything starts with a belief. Only if you believe in yourself, your ability to do certain things, you'll think, behave, and act accordingly. No Belief- No Action. The formula is to make a loop i.e., Strong belief >> Massive Actions >> Better Results, which lead to >> even stronger beliefs.

The 3 biggest challenges in building a strong belief are Fear, Uncertainty and Doubt (call them FUDs) and while they are in your head, you'll never believe that you can think differently and come out with creative solutions.

You have to **develop two powerful levers of belief**. (1) That you are capable of doing your part of the job; (2) That something inside of you makes you talented or capable as any other person in the world.

Develop powerful beliefs by Using Tick-Tock Technique. For every negative belief- put them in a "tick" column, and counter them with a strong objective argument in the "tock" column.

Use self-affirmations in the form of "commitment" that makes them feel real and help you develop a new belief system.

Surround yourself with people who evoke a sense of faith in you, and minimize spending time with the people are negative in nature.

Always remember more of your past successes than reminiscing about your failures, because where focus goes, there energy flows.

Chapter 4: Preset Challenge and Install Routines to Start Thinking Differently

****

"Life is meant to be a challenge, because challenges are what make you grow."

~Manny Pacquiao

We talked about the significance of building the inner infrastructure by learning techniques to strengthen our belief system in the previous chapter.

But here comes a challenge. We can't stay positive and rocking all the time. We have contrasting thoughts oscillating between positive and negative ones.

According to human psychology, we are bound to experience happiness and sadness as crest and troughs in the ocean. We have to face outside world daily, meet different sets of people, be it family members, your manager or subordinates, your friends, etc. Everyone has their own set of thoughts, behaviors, and not everyone who comes across you is guaranteed to offer you positive vibes. Therefore, you are bound to face negative thinking, unsupportive behavior, and unwanted reactions from your environment.

Therefore, we all need something that triggers the positive behavior that's conducive to innovative thinking. Not only that, we need to design our routines in such a way that they help us get our creative juices out more often every single day.

How do we create those triggers?

It's by creating some external stimulant that gives our mind a challenge to get excited about. Let's talk about how setting a challenge works wonder and how to get started about it.

Set Challenge to Prompt Out of The Box Thinking.

Set a Specific Challenge

Tricking your mind with a specific challenge to be solved is much more rewarding than simply trying to think innovatively without any specific objective.

Take an example. You won't be motivated to drive your car faster unless you have a clarity of destination and the specific time you plan to reach there. By specifying the destination and the time needed to reach there, your mind would understand the challenge. Now, it will be consistently aligned with the end objective of driving faster to reach the destination in time.

Similarly, our mind doesn't come into full action unless we give it a specific challenge to address. Let's talk about how to identify the type of challenge and how to transmit it to our minds in three simple steps:

Step 1: Identify what exactly is the problem

Most people see problems as a bad thing to be avoided, but that's not the case with creative thinkers. According to them, a problem is nothing but an opportunity clothed in disguise. They perceive problems as an opportunity to take action to make the most out of it. Since you are reading this book about thinking out of the box, it already means that you are open to exploring new ideas or things.

Your problem should be about something that is really meaningful to you such that finding the solution will help you immensely in getting closer to your goals.

If you don't have a sincere interest in finding a solution to the problem, then it would lack the necessary glue that sticks your mind to the problem for a longer time.

Therefore, identify your problem (oh, I mean identify your opportunity).

Step 2: The next step is to it convert the problem into **specific challenges.**

Let's understand this by way of an example. Assume you want to double the sales of your product or service in the next 6 months, that's the identification of the problem.

You can convert the problem into challenges by asking specific questions like:

- What are the various platforms or channels that you need to exploit to increase sales?
- Do you need to approach someone for help or collaboration that can improve your sales?
- Would the endorsement of someone with authority improve your chances of success?

You can add as many questions that come up in relation to finding a solution to your problem.

These questions will offer you a set of challenges for your mind to find answers to. Once you have a specific set of questions and you know that answers to those questions will lead to resolution of the problem, your mind will take them as challenges that need to be overcome to offer solutions to the problem.

If you have identified a meaningful problem, you have already provided your mind an explicit reason or purpose to stay committed to generating the ideas.

You have now given specific challenges to your mind. From here starts the process of generating the ideas.

Step 3: The last but the most important step is to **assign very compelling reasons** to your mind for coming out with an idea. Before you decide to solve a challenge, make a list of benefits, rewards, be it financials, emotions or otherwise that you want to achieve by solving the problem:

- What are the direct benefits? It could be money, recognition in the market, your branding, etc.

- Does it offer you a better living of your lifestyle by saving your time and efforts in some manner?

- Do you get opportunities to collaborate with some other people in your industry that gives you indirectly more business opportunities?

- What are the indirect benefits? It could be the acquisition of new skills, knowledge, more freedom to spend time on the things that you love to do, etc.

- How would you emotionally feel after getting the solution to your challenges?

To reiterate, the more specific and meaningful the benefits and rewards are to you, the more your mind will be emotionally charged up to generate new ideas.

Now take a pause reading.

Think about your specific and a meaningful problem, convert it into very specific challenges by asking questions, and imagine the rewards you will get by solving the problem.

Do this exercise for the next 10 to 15 minutes or so in a focused and undistracted environment. You will get the first-hand experience, and I'm confident that you'll attract plenty of new ideas.

Now let's move to the next point, which is going to help you find answers to your challenges from a variety of resources.

Openness to Experiences Invites Creativity

Whenever we perform any routine nature of tasks, there is a set of neural pathways that get formed by the regular firing of similar types of neurons. Your brain simply uses the existing neural pathways it has already created. Firing of neurons requires energy, and our brain wants to conserve as much energy as it can to use it for survival purpose. Hence, creating and following a set of neural pathways makes the brain's job easier, and it expends less energy.

Neurons have a 'memory' for existing neural pathways (this is how we learn), and will revert to these unless trained to do otherwise.

Therefore, to get the most out of our brains, we need to train our minds to create a different and new set of neural pathways by training the areas of the brain that we use less in our typical activities.

And that's the very basis of the science of neuroplasticity of the brain. Our brains are malleable to the extent we expose them to different sets of environment, people, and behaviors. Exposing ourselves to different environment and behaviors lets neurons in different parts of brain fire, and thus, wire with each other and that in turn forms new neural pathways. This enables us to develop new skills, new ways of thinking, and behaviors.

In the end, the out of box thinking or creativity is nothing but the ability to produce the work that is novel (original, unique), and useful.

Also, as shown by one study[a], when looking at a person's creative ability, a trait named ***"Openness to experience"*** was considered as one of the most consistent traits of creative ability.

Openness is closely related to having a flexible cognitive style when approaching problems, that is, being able to "think outside the box" and not being tied to any one perspective. Openness and flexibility, in turn, are related to activating the imagination to think of how things could be, not just how they are.

While we can do a range of things to train our brains to be creative, openness to experience is one of the easiest things to develop. If we willingly try newer things, we will train our brain to develop new neural pathways way more frequently.

How Openness to Music Helps Enhance Neuroplasticity and Thus Your Cognitive Abilities?

The purpose of neuroplasticity is to break away from the existing routine pattern.

One of the best ways to increase neuroplasticity, which is very important for boosting your creative thinking, is to learn any musical instrument.

Nina Kraus, a professor of neurobiology states that active engagement with musical sounds not only enhances neuroplasticity but also enables the nervous system to provide the stable scaffolding of meaningful patterns so important to learning.

Learning and playing it engages a whole range of brain functions, as we need to visualize the music, move our hands and arms, listen to the feedback, and generate an emotional response, all things together. Your mind gets more open to experiences from moment to moment while playing a musical instrument.

Though learning any musical instrument is a faster way to increase neuroplasticity due to the benefits it provides, but that is not the only way to do it.

The idea is to increase the openness of our minds to a new set of experiences, and that includes the versatility of experiences. Let me help you by stating a few ways you can experience new things:

- By trying a new route to your workplace.
- Eating food at different restaurants with different cuisines.
- Playing different types of sports.
- Listening to and playing with kids often.
- Join different meetup groups, where you interact with different sets of people.
- Reading books on subjects not related to your subjects.
- Traveling to different places and understanding their culture and lifestyle.

Anything which gives you a different experience beyond your routine will help you build your creativity and let you generate more ideas.

Daily Routines To Nurture Creativity Day After Day

Our habits and routines enable us to put the most important things on autopilot. Enough repetition of any activity sets a new program in your mind, and once that program is set, you don't need to exercise much of willpower to keep going.

In this section, we will talk about key routines that are well-researched and scientifically proven to boost your creative thinking skills.

Regular Exercising

Exercise tops the chart when it comes to powerful routines for enhancing creative thinking and amassing wonderful new ideas.

Developing a routine of exercising 3 to 5 times a week, not only keeps your body healthy, fit, and strong, it's also equally important for your mental health. Let's understand some neuroscience behind exercise and creativity.

Exercise activates a compound in your brain that boosts cognitive performance. This compound is called Brain-Derived Neurotrophic Factor, or BDNF for short. BDNF is responsible for increasing the connection between your different brain cells. It helps in growing your hippocampus portion, responsible for memory. BDNF helps you with forward thinking, learning, and increases your creative processes.

Dr. Mark Hyman, a functional medicine practitioner who has researched deeper into this brain chemical, explains how exercise is one of the most important things you can do to generate more of BDNF and thus, enhance your brain and memory. Memory plays a very important role in creativity because as we all know, creativity is nothing but making different permutation and combination of various ideas.

The more you remember your experience through your memory, the more you are able to form new ideas. Someone rightly said that creativity is nothing but a fusion of memory and imagination.

Therefore, the more BDNF you can generate in your brain, the better will be your ability to think out of the box.

A study[3] showed that aerobic exercise caused a 32% increase in BDNF in adult human males while BDNF decreased by 13% in people who chose a sedentary lifestyle.

How to let our brains secrete more BDNF for enhanced creativity?

Strength training increases BDNF, but only for a few minutes post-workout. But as one study[4] found, vigorous intensity cardiovascular exercise (80% heart rate) with a 40 minutes exercise offered the greatest possibility of significant BDNF elevation. You can do running, swimming, walking, or any other cardiovascular exercise.

Also, another research was carried out by Stanford University[5], revealing that simply walking has significant benefits to creative thinking; even sustaining for a little while after the walk. Walking either indoors on a treadmill, or outdoors in the fresh air both appear to produce twice as many creative responses compared to a person sitting down.

No wonder why Steve Jobs used to have walking meetings, and similarly, Mark Zuckerberg holds a meeting while walking on foot.

Taking a Shower

A shower is a place where you get ideas shower too. You might have already heard most CEOs often quoting that their best ideas come when they are taking a bath in showers. Archimedes ran out naked after taking a bath in a shower shouting "Eureka," when he got the answer to the problem he was searching for days and weeks.

Why is it so?

Alice Flaherty, one of the most renowned neuroscientists researching creativity, informs that one of the most important ingredients for enhancing creativity is dopamine, a neurotransmitter that plays an active role in the centers of pleasure and reward in the brain. The more dopamine is released, the more creative you are. Taking a shower makes us feel great and relaxed and immediately increases the level of dopamine in our brain. The chances of having great ideas when we have higher dopamine in our brain are a lot higher.

While the population of the world takes one bath a day as a part of morning personal hygiene before getting to work, it's advisable to have more of this relaxing ritual. You can take a shower before going to sleep to have a better sleep or if your schedule permits, one in the evening as well.

Get more of dopamine many times a day to invite creativity through this simple routine.

Mindfulness Meditation Improves Creativity

Studies[6] have associated mindfulness meditation with many cognitive and psychological benefits, such as:

- Improved task concentration
- Sustained attention, empathy, and introspection
- Enhanced memory
- Improved learning

And many of these benefits are central to creativity.

There are two types of mindfulness meditations, and we need to understand which one is beneficial for innovative thinking:

1) Open-monitoring, which involves observing and noting phenomena in the present moment and keeping attention flexible and unrestricted, and

2) Focused attention, which stresses concentrating on a single object, such as breathing, and ignoring other stimuli.

A 2012 study[7] conducted by Lorenza Colzato proved that it was open-monitoring meditation that was far more stimulating the divergent thinking i.e., thinking out of the box. On the other hand, the focused attention mediation is more strongly related to convergent thinking, which is important for narrowing options and formulating a workable solution.

Another set of studies[8] conducted by another Dutch psychologist, Matthijs Baas, showed the importance of mindfulness in improving the observation skills, the ability to observe internal phenomena (such as bodily sensations, thoughts, and emotions) and external stimuli (sights, sounds, smells, etc.).

One major finding of the above studies was that high observation scores were the only consistently reliable predictor of creativity. That skill, which is enhanced by open-monitoring meditation, not only improved working memory, it also increased cognitive flexibility and reduced cognitive rigidity—all of which are critical to the creative process. According to Baas, the ability to observe is closely related to openness to experience, a personality trait that several studies have shown to be one of the most robust indicators of creative success.

How to do Open-Monitoring Meditation?

John M. DeCastro, from the Contemplative Studies[9] blog, explains a very detailed and self-explanatory manner about how to do open monitoring mindfulness meditation. You'll find this excerpt helpful to get started with open-monitoring meditation.

Here is how to get started:

"[In open monitoring mindfulness meditation].....we open up our awareness to everything that we're experiencing regardless of its origin.

We still <u>pay attention to the sensations associated with breathing but open it up further to all bodily sensations</u>, including the feelings from the skin of touch, coldness or hotness, the pressure exerted by gravity on our rear ends sitting on the chair or cushion, tingling sensations on the skin and elsewhere, sensations from muscles and joints, sensations of balance and body position, the subtle feeling of our heart beating with the consequent blood pressure surges, and the feelings from our internal organs such as from our stomachs, bowels, bladder, etc.

In addition, <u>we open up our awareness and pay attention to external stimuli</u>, sights, sounds, tastes, and smells. Even with our eyes closed, we can perceive visual stimulation, some due to light penetrating the eyelids and some due to spontaneous activity in the neural systems underlying vision. In open monitoring meditation, we let it all into awareness and don't try to focus on any one thing or exclude anything.

The openness extends to thoughts. Although we don't try to engage in thinking, thoughts will inevitably arise anyway. In open monitoring meditation, we don't try to stop them. We just watch them rising up and falling away."

You should make open-monitoring a part of your daily routine. However, if you engage in open monitoring mindfulness meditation before you start your most important projects, it will prime your mind and connect everything going into your subconscious mind and you'll be able to generate more ideas.

Be Careful with your Television watching or other Distractive Routines

Watching television is the mental and emotional equivalent of eating junk food. You may feel a temporary form of recovery by watching television, but it is rarely nutritious, and it is easy to consume too much. Researchers, such as Mihaly Csikszentmihalyi, have found that prolonged television watching is actually correlated with increased anxiety and low-level depression.

For any creativity enthusiast, you can't make connections between different ideas if you are always busy watching TV, smartphone, or engaged in any other kind of distraction. Your mind needs some space or rest. If you're constantly plugged into distractions, it will be much harder for your brain to rest and make connections.

You should be either producing or rejuvenating. That's how your day should be structured. Don't get me wrong. I'm not against winding down after long work hours. You need time to rejuvenate and re-energize your mind to again get into another productive day but Binge watching TV or Netflix for hours is definitely not the best way to rejuvenate. You can read some fiction book, or maybe control watching any show for say 30 minutes a day (but be careful not to let yourself glued to the TV for hours once you get started).

I personally have disconnected my cable connection DTH (direct to home connection) and personally use internet to watch something based on my knowledge requirements and don't simply get misguided by a television channel about what to watch.

How to put all this together?

I definitely didn't want to overwhelm you with many habits and routines that you find difficult to even get started. Therefore, I chose specifically only those routines that can directly help you in thinking creative solutions to your biggest problems.

Above routines are a few you can easily accommodate in your daily life without any major compromises with your existing commitments.

I think you can easily accommodate taking one or more showers in your routine besides your regular one shower in the morning. If you already take 2-3 showers a day, that's wonderful, and you might already be seeing results in terms of dopamine rush in your brain. Exercise is something that is a must anyway for physical health and avoiding ailments, so why not use it to get a double advantage of increasing our creativity. All innovative thinking comes from the mind, so using a few techniques of mindfulness is definitely the best return on your time invested, so it definitely makes sense.

I do all these practices regularly in my life and I see the difference in the level of my creative thinking and generation of new ideas.

I hope you will start implementing these routines in your daily life and see the magic with your own eyes.

Now, let's move to the most awaited sections of this book, where I'll tell you the effective techniques to generate ideas on demand. I'll see you in the next chapter with effective techniques to generate ideas on demand.

Chapter 4: Key Takeaways

In this chapter, you learned how you could trigger creativity and further make creativity come to you more often through some daily routines.

Giving a specific and meaningful challenge opens up our mind to generate more ideas than to simply sit and wait for ideas, as your mind wants to be sure of the rewards of being creative.

Alongside the specific challenge to generate ideas, **you need to increase your openness to experiences in your life**. The more experiences you take, the more it will boost your brain's neuroplasticity, and that in turn, will offer more creativity to your brain.

Learning **some musical instruments has been proved by science to increase your creative abilities** more. A few routines can be most important to create more ideas on autopilot basis.

Exercise improves BDNF that is important for memory and creativity. Get more BDNF through intense cardio exercises.

Take Showers: **Taking showers has been proved to generate more dopamine**. The higher the dopamine, the more the possibility of getting creative ideas. Therefore, take more showers.

Follow Open Monitoring Mindfulness Meditation. This will open your

observation skills – i.e., observing your body and organs from inside, observing outside sounds, smells, and also observing your thoughts, feelings, etc. alongside. The more your observe, the more your divergent thinking skills improve.

Finally, cut off your cable T.V. connection and watch something you find necessary and important for your mind.

Chapter 5: Effective Techniques to Think Out of Box

****

"You can't use up creativity. The more you use, the more you have. "

~Maya Angelou

So far, you've learned about the mechanism to design your inner infrastructure. You've also understood the significance of crafting specific challenges and developing a few key routines that best support creative thinking.

With suitable infrastructure within and proper designing of the environment from outside, you are now fully geared up to start learning the best ways to generate creative ideas more often.

So let's get started with:

Feed Your Mind Immensely

Idea generation can't happen in a vacuum. There has to be something underlying.

We already talked in the previous section that you need to identify your problem, and then define it in the form of a challenge before you can invite the solutions. Defining your challenge narrows down the path you have to go. But merely doing that doesn't get you started to invite the idea.

You've to do a lot of groundwork. As you will see later in the book that there are in fact no new ideas, rather they are the combination of the existing ideas.

Therefore, the first step or the groundwork required for idea generation is to feed your head with a variety of ideas, because these ideas have to play with each other in order to generate more and different ideas.

Creative thinkers need to feed their head with a lot of new information and ideas. As Gore Vidal, a prolific writer puts it, *"The brain that doesn't feed itself eats itself."*

You can't undermine the importance of exposing your mind to different ideas. Your mind needs a lot – really a lot more information than you think before you start generating ideas on demand. That's why they say knowledge is power. You need to feed your mind enough, and with a variety of information for it to process the different ingredients and turn into an idea recipe that's uniquely generated from your mind.

Let's talk about some of the ideas to pump your mind when you read:

> a. **Study a variety of literature**. Don't always stick to reading something that is related to your profession or industry only. You may

find reading a different type of literature difficult or unrelated, but this will only open you up to a new set of ideas that you can tweak and use in your domain. That's where your idea will be different from others because others' ideas might be restricted to the preset concepts of your domain, while you are choosing the best practices from other domains and crafting it again according to your industry.

b. **Select your reading material carefully**. Ask yourself whether this reading is going to provide enough exercise to develop the creativity of your brain. Precisely, the reading should stimulate your mind and create the fertile ground for generating ideas. You should be cautioned that you don't merely slip into reading what solely entertains you instead of educating you. Entertainment also has a place in life, but when we talk about feeding your head, it doesn't take the driver's seat – so you have to be careful about the selection of reading material.

c. **Take notes while reading**: Write notes everywhere in the book to identify and distinguish different facts. When you write notes in the book with your hands, that gives a signal to the brain that it's important. And also, you summarize the finding for your own deeper understanding of the subject (this applies equally when you are writing in an ebook format- and most ebook readers have the option to take note). That way, you start building a vocabulary of different ideas that will fire neurons in your brain to connect with other ideas and generate something new.

d. **Read biographies**: Biographies are really the treasure-houses of ideas. You start relating the experience of that person with your own life experiences, and then it opens up new ideas before you in that particular situation. The more biographies you read, the more you'll see the life stories and turning points in the lives of people you admire. This itself will prompt the generation of new ideas.

e. **Read how to books on different subjects**: Exercise your mind by manipulating the ideas of others used in another domain and convert them into your new ideas. The solutions people had already adopted for one type of problem can be adopted in a different kind of situation as well. The more you read about "How To's" of different sorts, the more they will open up a new set of information that you can later combine with other ideas and create new solutions.

f. Read magazines on a variety of subjects like science, business, politics, fashion, and others to get an idea of the current trends in different industries. The more you know of the trends in different fields, the wider will be your net of ideas to implement.

g. If you are into business, try to hire people who are successful in other industries. They will be able to look at your industry from a fresh perspective that you could never have imagined on your own. In my past experience, I worked with a reputed media company. I remember them hiring someone from the FMCG industry and more particularly, from the packaged edible oil industry to oversee the media company's advertising and promotion strategies. While the experience of a new hire in the oil industry *per se* would not help much, but it certainly helps to get a fresh perspective of a person who had successfully implemented various concepts in a different area of business.

h. Attend as many business conferences, seminars or events as you can, related to your profession and then some others as well.

i. Do Content Analysis: You need to analyze the different form of content passing through your desk or otherwise. Here is how you should do content analysis:

- Scan your junk mails before discarding – this will help you get an idea of advertising trends, marketing approach, new products or services coming out in the market.
- When you are traveling or on the road, look for different newspapers,

magazines, local radio stations. This will give you a perspective on the local trends, business opportunities, people's lifestyle, some better marketing or advertising approach. Later on, you can use them in your area.

If you do all of the above exercises, you'll never be short of ideas, as your head is filled with new framework from the versatile background. In the writing world, people talk about writers' block. In effect, most of the time, this is the lack of proper research and scarcity of information, which is the first step that's needed for letting your brain connect with different parts of the brain to get more ideas.

Novelist Vikram Seth[10], rose to literary superstar by landing a publishing deal that offered him $ 1.1 million advances. But not many people know that he once found himself trapped into a writer's block after writing the first hundred pages of a story set in post-independence India. In spite of his best efforts to move the story forward, he couldn't make any further progress in the story. So he started doubting his writing abilities.

This was until one fine day when he realized he had overlooked the real problem: he simply didn't know enough about post-independence India period. Once he understood this, Seth switched from writing to research, reading old newspapers, visiting key places, and interviewing people who had lived through the era. This gave him so much material that his planned short novel grew into a huge 1366 pages novel titled *Suitable Boy,* which very well skyrocketed his literary career.

Therefore, feeding your mind is the first step to pump your mind. This is the foundational work, and you can't generate any ideas if you don't have enough information stored in your head currently.

Idea Fusion to Generate Idea Babies

We hear all the time that a new idea could change someone's life. Every day, we see some new product or technology coming up to surprise and change the way we do certain things.

Facebook changed the way people socially connected with each other just around a decade ago. Similarly, email disrupted the formal communication in the business world with the lightning speed of communication to many people simultaneously.

In the business world, we keep seeing some startup getting millions of dollars of funding by generating some novel concept to solve some problems.

If after getting to know about one or more innovation daily, you hear someone saying, "there are no new ideas," how will you react?

Obviously, you will discard this as a stupid statement. But what if such statement comes from one of the most creative people in history?

Mark Twain, the famous author of The Adventures of Tom Sawyer and many other creative works accredited to his name and known for his humor, vivid details, and memorable, once said that:

"There is no such thing as a new idea. It is impossible*. We simply take a lot of old ideas and put them into a sort of mental kaleidoscope. We give them a turn, and they make new and curious combinations. We keep on turning and making new combinations indefinitely; but they are the same old pieces of colored glass that have been in use through all the ages."*

I personally agree with this statement.

Of course, on the face of it, everything happening around us seems to be quite novel based on new ideas or thoughts, but they are nothing but a well-incubated fusion of different ideas only.

Generating a ground-breaking new idea like getting a spaceship to a different planet for tourism, as you read earlier in the book, is definitely a way more difficult and riskier project, but every idea doesn't have to be like that. And that's good news for everyone because if you could just calmly observe all the existing ideas in your head, and just try some different combinations here and there, you can also come out with any new combination of ideas.

Was Facebook a brand new earth-shattering idea?

No, there were already Friendster and Myspace. But Facebook made a different combination of features, user interface, and engagement algorithms that made them a highly profitable business idea.

Was Google a novel idea to become a hit in 1996 as a search engine?

No, Lycos (1993) and Yahoo (1994) and few others were pre-existing. But again, Google applied some more improvements over the previous ones. For example, adding the feature of filtering out the relevancy and utility from the user's perspective and adding some other features available, so it became a grand success.

Similarly, Apple's iPhone was not the first smartphone; rather, the first smartphone was created more than a decade ago by IBM in 1992.

It's not always a brand new innovative idea that flourishes versus the people who make improvements over the previous innovations. Rather, the people or companies who improve on the existing projects get better chances of success.

There was a case study done on 50 different products to compare the failure rate amongst the startups, who were the first movers, i.e., who created an entirely new product or market, and the improvers who introduced something different and better than the original movers. The study concluded that the first movers had an average failure rate of 47%, as compared to the improvers, whose failure rate was 8% only. Also, logistically, it's much easier to improve on somebody else's idea than it is to create something entirely new from scratch. Therefore, to be creative thinker, you don't have to be first. You just have to be different and better.

How fusion of different idea works?

Let's look at a few examples of how the fusion of multiple ideas triggered the origination of transformative ideas.

The first example of fusion of ideas comes from Sylvan Goldman, an American businessman, and inventor of the shopping cart, who came up with something different that no one else had thought of before 1937. He observed that in stores, people buy only as many grocery items as they can hold their hands. Once they realize they are not able to hold more products, they don't buy further. Here is what he did. He took one chair, put wheels under it, and then put a basket on the seat. This was the birth of the shopping cart, now a universal phenomenon. It's a great example of synthesizing ideas and relationship between unrelated things – like a chair, wheel, and basket and combining them to form a moving shopping cart.

Let's take another real-life example.

Scott Adams, author of How to *Fail at Almost Everything and Still Win Big,* describes his story of coming up with an idea of starting Dilbert comic strip. He worked in the corporate world for many years, so he knew about the non-resourceful gossiping and office politics prevalent in the corporate environment. That was his one idea. On the other hand, he had a flair for drawing art- by cartooning. So he came out with a combination of both ideas to draw a cartoon series where he would portray the meaninglessness of the corporate world politics through a cartoon, and that was the beginning of highly successful Dilbert series on the ground.

Justin Musk (Elon Musk's ex-wife) summed up the significance of idea fusion in the words below:

*"Choose one thing and become a master of it. Choose a second thing and become a master of that. When you become a master of two worlds (say, engineering and business), you can bring them together in a way that will a) introduce hot ideas to each other, so they can have idea sex **and make idea babies that no one has seen before**, and b) create a competitive advantage because you can move between*

worlds, speak both languages, connect the tribes, **mash the elements to spark fresh creative insight** *until you wake up with the epiphany that changes your life."*

Hope the above examples helped you, made you think about the different ideas already floating in your head.

Now, let's see how the mechanism of fusion of ideas plays out in our minds.

Generating ideas is the capacity to synthesize rather than to analyze. It's all about seeing the relationship between unrelated things; to see the broad pattern instead of seeing the specific answers, and to invent something new by combining something that wasn't paired by someone else earlier.

As you have already learned in the previous section, idea synthesis is the right hemisphere's work, while the left hemisphere is more responsible for doing analytical work.

One of the best ways to fuse ideas is to do it by way of mind mapping, a technique invented by Tony Buzan, a brain expert, and author. A mind map is a diagram used to visually organize information. A mind map is hierarchical and shows relationships among pieces of the whole. It is created around a single concept, drawn as an image in the center of a blank page (i.e., your key challenge), to which representations of ideas such as images, words, and parts of words are added as branches to the central idea.

You begin with your challenge or problem and start drawing branches of interconnected ideas related to that topic that can be shown as words or images. Once you have multiple ideas appearing on paper in front of you, you start to build connection, and this will help you come out with a unique combination that you couldn't have thought of, had you not been able to see all of them together at one place.

Do SCAMPER to get Loads of Ideas Instantly

The SCAMPER method offers you a checklist for idea-spurring questions. It provides a structured way of assisting students to think out of the box.

SCAMPER method was proposed by Alex Faickney Osborn, an advertising executive and author in 1953, and was further developed in 1971 by Bob Eberle in his book, *SCAMPER: Games for Imagination Development.*

The seven-letter acronym describes how you can generate multiple ideas by dividing your challenge or project into different stages and brainstorming ideas by asking the following questions about each stage.

- S = **Substitute** something
- C = **Combine** it with something else
- A = **Adapt** something to it
- M = **Modify** or Magnify it

- P = **Put it** to some different use
- E = **Eliminate** something
- R = **Reverse** Engineer it.

How to use SCAMPER Technique

Step 1: You have to isolate your challenge into different parts or stages.

Step 2: After that, apply each of the seven elements of the SCAMPER method to each of the stages of your project for asking questions and generating ideas.

To help you understand the practical application of this technique, let's experiment this with a hypothetical example.

Let's assume that your challenge is to start a profitable café franchise business.

The first step is to break down your challenge into various stages. The following could be the probable stages for this business.

1. *Researching* a café franchise or brand that's well known in a nearby area, where people prefer to spend time for meetings, work, or just for having a good coffee. You definitely would want to assure there is a good probability of footfall as well as the franchisor offers you a profitable revenue share.

2. *Negotiating a good deal* with the franchisor and sign the agreement.

3. *Finding out the best location* for your business and getting the best deal for lease.

4. *Advertising and inviting customers to visit your café.*

Now, let's pick up one of the stages of your project and ask SCAMPER questions for generating more ideas. Let's look at inviting customers to your upcoming café and ask yourself the following questions:

- **What advertising platform can I _substitute_ for my existing ways of advertising and inviting customers?**

Can you substitute the existing way of circulating pamphlets in the newspapers and other offline magazines that comparatively costs more money with something like social media advertising on Facebook, Instagram, or other active social media platforms?

- **What else can you _combine_ with your existing means of advertising?**

Maybe you could give referral coupons to the people visiting your café so that they can share them online with their friends that offer them some discount on the next visit, as well as offer discount to the new customers.

- **What else can I _adapt_ or copy from some of the existing business' advertising model?**

Do you need to think of offering some other features like other cafes offer i.e., free internet connection for the first 2 hours or a discount coupon for next two visits for first-time visitors?

- **How can I _modify or magnify_ the way I advertise?**

Maybe you can think of inviting some local celebrity or influencer to your café (that might cost you money), and letting that celebrity spread the message on his social media followings, so you can magnify the impact of your advertisement.

- *How can I _put_ my marketing efforts to some other use?*

You can think of using your marketing efforts in converting those initial leads into your regular customers by offering some monthly discounted offers, so you ensure that you have a recurring income generated.

- **What can you _eliminate_ from your existing way of inviting customers?**

Maybe you can totally do away with expensive means of advertising to use that money in better and viral ways of communication.

- **What could be _reversed_ or _re-engineered_ in your way of inviting customers to your place?**

Think about whether there could be some way where instead of you advertising, your customers do a free advertising for you i.e., by word of mouth. For example, whosoever shares the spending of their moments at the café over Instagram or Facebook by tagging the café social media page, would be instantly offered a 20% discount on their orders. School or college students generally get excited with this, and they can spread the word about your café faster. That way, you will get tons of advertisement done by your customers through word of mouth or referral advertising. This will also turn the algorithm of social media platform to your favor, because of the higher level of engagement on your social media page and this can significantly reduce your ad spend as you get more organic reach.

Okay, you just saw how the SCAMPER method worked to generated multiple ideas by forcing a specific set of questions to generate a variety of ideas.

I don't have any plans to open a café as of now, but since I'm writing this section while sitting in a café, I picked up the example of opening a Café, and you see how this SCAMPER method started generating all those good ideas by triggering little prompts. Moreover, in the example, we used this technique on just one stage of your business idea, and if you apply this on each stage, there is going to be a flood of ideas.

Actually, your mind has an unlimited potential that needs to be tapped by asking the right set of questions and the SCAMPER method does the very same thing by asking different set of questions in an intelligent manner. SCAMPER offers subtle cues or triggers that trigger your mind to come out with various alternatives.

How to implement SCAMPER in your personal or work life?

Just think about one of the meaningful projects that you want to succeed in by applying innovative and creative thinking. After you have finalized the project, divide the project into as many small steps as it makes sense to do in a way that each step can be ascertained separately.

Now, take any one stage of your important project and apply each of the SCAMPER questions on that step, and keep noting down different ideas on your note pad or laptop.

Apply SCAMPER on each of the methods, and keep scribbling all the ideas coming to you.

Once you are done, start looking at the ideas you have generated. I'm sure you will produce way more ideas than you do get by just ordinary thinking. Try this out on your own to see the difference.

Now with that, let's move to another technique to think out of the box.

How Multi-tasking This Way Improves Creativity

There is enough research now that multi-tasking is not good when we talk about increasing productivity and focus.

According to the late Stanford neuroscientist, Clifford Nass[11], multitasking should really be called "multi-switching," because the human brain does not have the capacity to focus on several tasks at once. If you are multi-tasking, you are simply switching back and forth between tasks very quickly, which almost always results in a loss of productivity.

He further explained that people that do multitask are not able to filter irrelevancy. They lose their ability to prioritize things properly and end up doing things that don't require to be done in the first place.

But there is a different type of multi-tasking that is in fact recommended when it comes to giving space to let the creative thinking emerge. Let me explain by citing some examples of some of the smartest people to understand this different type of multi-tasking.

In the year 1905, Albert Einstein presented four different work projects namely his famous theory of general science of relativity (that won him a Nobel Prize), quantitative theory of Brownian motions; the famous e=mc2 (energy equals mass times the speed of light squared); and the theory of Photoelectric effect.

Four major projects presented in one year only.

How did he make it possible?

In fact, Einstein always kept working on different types of projects at the same time. He used to start multiple projects as they came to his mind. However, he worked long enough on one project and then used to take a break from one project and then started to work on a different project.

Take another example. Michael Crichton, the director and producer of movie *Jurassic Park,* worked on the movie and alongside that, he wrote novels and one more non-fiction book.

What's happening here?

No, don't get it wrong. None of them were juggling between tasks of different nature all at the same time. They didn't believe in that type of multi-tasking. Rather, they were doing slow multi-tasking.

Why do the top creators keep switching between the different types of projects? Or to put it differently, how does slow multi-tasking helps get more done?

Here are the reasons:

- It helps them keep working on other projects if they get stuck in one project, and that way, they keep making progress in another project.

For example, in 1915, Einstein was exhausted in his theory of general relativity, so he switched his attention to a different project. The switching of attention to another project gave him enough time in his head to incubate the ideas and let a solution emerge to his theory of relativity.

Later, when he switched back to the main project, he was refreshed and could look at his problems in an entirely different way.

- Switching between different projects slowly satisfies the need of novelty for the human brain. The human mind craves for uncertainty in a positive manner, so changing the project keeps the mind excited and focused for longer periods.

- Also, this type of slow multi-tasking is like cross training of our mind. Compare this slow multi-tasking with preparing for half marathon.

You don't always keep running every day. On some days, you don't run and rather do cross-training to give the necessary stretch to your body as well relax your leg muscles. The shifting from intense focus in one project to a different project works like a cross-training for your mind, and when you jump to your original task, you go much refreshed in the new task.

- Also, if you can learn to do one thing well, it helps you to do other things also well.

Therefore, if we want to do something in a much better way, we should often get disconnected with the main project for some time.

There was a study conducted where it was revealed that top scientists switched their topic on an average of 43 times out of their first 100 research papers.

I know one lawyer in India, Ajay Kumar, who is a journalist and a Supreme Court lawyer in India, but he started his own TV Channel recently. He is authoring a book on collection of life stories of different people, and he also hosts a talk show where he invites people on his show to let the audience know their inspiring stories. This is a good example of slow multi-tasking and working on different projects all together.

American choreographer, Twyal Tharp, who has worked in different areas, danced to different music, written three books – in a way she is a slow multi-tasker, says *"you have to be all things, why exclude? You have to be everything."*

To ensure that different tasks don't overwhelm her, she prepares a cardboard box for different nature of projects that come to her mind. She writes a name on the project and then tosses DVDs, books, articles, magazines, news release, everything in that box, that is relevant and inspire her creativity. That way, she doesn't have to worry about losing any idea as well as she can start working on the project whenever she is ready.

You can notice that by doing the slow multi-tasking, she never misses any creative thought, nor she has to filter her creative thought only restricted to her single ongoing project at that time.

You never know when you get excited about a different thing in your life, and then those creative insights sparked through you will turn out to be a treasure.

How should you apply this technique to your life?

- Set up an introspection session with yourself. It's better to set up an appointment with yourself over a creativity walk, followed by creative journal writing. Probably some relax time on a holiday, maybe an hour or more, entirely with yourself without any distraction from outside.

- During your walking session, keep walking and think about the projects that you started earlier in life, but quitted sooner without giving your full shot to those projects. Maybe it's writing a book, or composing a song or a poem, or maybe contesting your residential society's election, where you could have contributed. You either didn't start or just left it immediately after you start assuming that it would distract you from your main project. Think through everything, and just keep recording short bullets of the ideas in your smartphone or notepad, whatever pops up. Maybe you just speak up and record the ideas in your phone recorder. Any of them could be your additional projects to work upon, so don't miss any point.

- An hour worth of walk is something that will sweat you out physically and stretch you mentally as well.

- Now after this walk, go home, relax a bit and get ready for your journaling session. Take a notebook and draw a small circle in the center of the page, with your name within the circle. Now, you need to draw a mind map of different projects branching out from the center in a way that you could draw out various sub-branches as well. For example, your branches could be:
  - Your contribution to the society
  - Physical Health.
  - Children growth-related projects
  - Your long desires for creating something that will contribute to the world.
  - And many more, as you can think of.

- Now, once you have listed some projects, take a few different color markers or pens and start highlighting with different colors with different categories, or else you may start giving them different identification marks with the same pen i.e., A1, A2, A3 etc. Your categories for different projects based on the time-frame you wanted to do could be
  - What you can start tomorrow.

- In a few weeks.
- In the next six months.
- Next year.
- Maybe sometime in the future.

This exercise will give you enough clarity about what could be the different projects that you can start doing along with your main projects already going on.

It might happen that you enroll in some music or dance class nearby or just start an online course on learning a new language tomorrow.

Try this out and let slow multi-tasking help you learn and achieve more while you are doing your main thing.

Become an Idea Machine- Set up Daily Idea Quota

Thomas Alva Edison had 1093 patents in his name in the US. He had set a clear objective for his team to have one minor invention every ten days and one major invention every six months.

James Altucher, in his book titled "Become an Idea Machine," recommends coming out with 10 new ideas every day. It doesn't matter if they are good or bad. The key is to exercise your "idea muscle," to keep it toned, and in great shape.

Developing ideas is also like building muscles. If you want to build muscles, you work out with heavier weights and stretch your muscles. You need to do the same with your ideas as well. Stretch your imagination and set a quota for yourself to come out with a specific number of ideas every day.

You'd ask what kind of ideas we are talking about

As I emphasized in the previous section, you need to have a clear problem and convert it into a challenge before you can invite new ideas. Therefore, the kind of ideas should be related to your core problems.

In the world of creativity, the greater the number of ideas, the better your choice will be. Quantity of ideas will lead to quality of ideas.

Making a habit of generating a fixed quota of ideas per day works better as it will discipline your mind to actively generate ideas rather than waiting for them to occur to you.

You can start with generating 5 ideas every day for a week in relation to your challenges. It will be hard initially, but once you start putting them down on paper, it will start connecting and lead you to better ideas.

Then look at the stock of ideas you generated over the week, and identify the winning ideas worth implementing for your important projects.

Chances are you may find one or two ideas that you can start implementing related to your most important projects.

Embrace Boredom to Let Ideas Emerge

Billionaire Sara Blakely, CEO, and founder of Spanx, offering a wide variety of slimming intimates, body shapers, hosiery, apparel, etc., stays very close by to her office, but still, she wakes up one hour earlier to drive her car aimlessly on different roads within the city for one hour every morning.

Why does she do this?

She responded in an interview[13] that her best ideas come when she is alone, child-free (she is a mother of four children under 10 years), and driving, letting her mind wander freely aimlessly.

Let's look at some more examples:

Newton was sitting idle under a tree doing nothing when an apple fell from the tree. His wandering mind suddenly noticed something that gave birth to the law of gravity.

Google allows its employees to spend 20% of their time as they want. They declared that the idea of Gmail.com originated from this "free" time.

Bill Gates started "Think Week" at Microsoft, where people spend time thinking and submitting innovative ideas to the leadership team at Microsoft.

What is so common about all these examples above?

It shows that the best ideas often come to us while doing nothing and just letting the mind reel and think whatever comes. In other words, big ideas pop up out of boredom.

Neuroscientists and psychologists have been doing their research on the subject, and they discovered that while we are getting bored, it activates the *default mode network* of the brain. In fact, there are two different types of network in the brain:

- Active Network
- Default Mode Network (DMN)

DMN is called the **imagination network** of the brain.

But the irony is that the modern technology doesn't leave any scope for any of us to get bored, as compared to even one generation before, who didn't have their eyes consistently glued to their smartphones.

I recall my early childhood when we had only one national television channel, and that broadcasted only for 3-5 hours every evening with just limited entertainment and news section. We waited for the entire week to just watch half an hour of songs telecasted on TV.

But compare the situation as of today, now, whenever you crave for some distractions, you have the luxury of endless feeds and notification on your Facebook, Twitter, Instagram, and many more. And the technology is so devised that they keep on showing more and more notifications like "You may like this also," or "People also viewed this," or "recommended read inspired by your views," or any other permutation or combination, solely to get you addicted to these apps. We keep on switching our attention from app to another one, from news article to another one, without realizing how much time had passed by.

In a nutshell, our minds are constantly in switch mode. Neuroscientist, Dr. Daniel Levitin, said that shifting your attention from one work to another – requires the brain to do a neurochemical switch that uses up the nutrients in the brain. If you keep on switching from one distraction to another, you are using up the glucose of your brain very fast. Glucose is the energy – the willpower of your mind.

The studies have proven that willpower is granted to you in limited supply every day. It is like a green 100% battery in your smartphone when you start your day. As the day passes by, you consume this battery by making phone calls, watching news updates or social media notifications or whatever you do with your phone. And by the evening, it is almost about to drain. Same happens with your level of energy when you keep switching it between different tasks.

One study conducted by Microsoft Corporation[13] showed that the immediate short term attention span of a human being is 8 seconds only, which is worse than the notoriously distracted goldfish (9 seconds).

The social media and video platform are being designed with a mission to glue your attention to them almost all the time.

Netflix promoted the term "Binge Watch." In one of the interviews, when asked about competitors, Netflix stated its biggest competitors are Facebook, YouTube, and **sleep**.

Also, codependency is no more about being dependent emotionally upon other human beings. Back in 2015, Manoush Zomorodi, author of *Bored and Brilliant: How Spacing Out Can Unlock Your Most Productive and Creative Self*, created a challenge with her audience about how to get disconnected from your smartphones. The challenge required people not to visit their favorite social media platforms that stole all their attention for the initial few days and subsequently were asked to delete that very app. One of the participants stated that he realized that his relationship with his phone was sort of codependent.

Think about a time in your everyday routine, when you just pick up the phone, maybe to check the time and end up realizing that you wasted forty minutes watching some other things. And you laughed out loud when you realized that you even forgot why you picked up the phone in the first place.

What is the solution to all this?

Therefore, the strategy here is to get ready for boredom for sometime during the day.

You can start with just thirty minutes of your time starting today.

Every day at some point in time during the day, you spend time with your phone. Think of a routine or schedule when you are forced by your habit to pick up the phone unconsciously to just scroll it. It could be in the evening when you are back from work or maybe just before you go to sleep. Whatever time it is, select the time.

Now today onwards, at that time, keep the phone, television, internet, or any device that gets your attention out in the world in a separate room or place, where you don't see it. And you sit in a separate room doing nothing, maybe you can just enjoy your tea or coffee or just sitting with your loved ones.

You will find a strong craving to go and check if there is some new picture posted by your friend or any new Whatsapp message popped up, but you have to control the urge and stay with yourself for that 30 minutes duration.

To help you smooth the transitioning process, keep a journal with you, where you can scribble anything. Just write whatever comes to your mind. Allow the different thoughts to pop up.

With some practice of sitting with yourself, you'll start to see your thoughts and emotions when they arise, and you'll start making connections between different ideas. And the chances are that you'll get to hear the best ideas for your important projects, that you can start implementing.

Therefore, you need to embrace boredom to let a new space form in your mind, where ideas can germinate, flourish, and soon you will start loving this boredom more and more.

Chapter 5 Key Takeaways

In this chapter, we learned about various techniques to think out of the box and generate more creative ideas.

1. **Feed your head** with a variety of information as a base before you can generate ideas. As Gore Vidal puts it, *"The brain that doesn't feed itself eats itself."* Study a variety of

literature, read biographies, read books on subjects other than yours to feed your head with enough information to let ideas germinate and flourish in your brain thereafter.

2. **Use Idea Fusion**: There are no new ideas, and often, most of the ideas are just a better combination or a useful improvement over the previous inventions. After you have fed your head with tons of ideas, it's the time to put all those ideas together. Mind mapping is a good technique that you can use to make all your different ideas come out on paper, so you can make better fusion of the ideas.

3. **Slow Multi-tasking improves creativity**. You should not switch between different tasks in your day to day work, but you should get yourself involved and working on different projects simultaneously. This gives some break from one project and gives your mind a thinking space to let better ideas form over time. Also, you get to make some progress on different projects together.

4. **Use SCAMPER Method**. This method equips you with 7 different ways you could ask questions from yourself. SCAMPER is an acronym, and each letter gives you a specific way to ask a question to generate ideas. It means:

   S = Substitute something

   C = Combine it with something else

   A = Adapt something to it

   M = Modify or Magnify it

   P = Put it to some different use

   E = Eliminate something

   R = Reverse Engineer it.

5. **Set a Daily quota for generating ideas**: You should fix a daily quota for yourself to generate at least 5 new ideas for your projects or challenges. You have to develop your idea muscle by practicing daily. The more the number of ideas you have, the better the quality of ideas you can select from them.

6. **Use Boredom to Invite Brilliance**: Getting bored means to not get continuously driven by your

frequent cravings and getting distracted often. If you are not doing anything, you'll feel bored. But the benefit of getting bored is it activates your default mode network (DMN) i.e., imagination network of your brain.

By always getting engaged in something puts your other network i.e., Active Network, in continuous mode, and not let DMN offer you the required insights generated by imagination. Therefore, make boredom a part of your life.

Chapter 6: Effective Strategies to Think Out of Box –continued

****

"The important thing for you is to be alert, to question, to find out, so that your own initiative may be awakened."

~Bruce Lee

In the previous chapter, you learned many ways to think out of the box. I hope you have found them useful and try to implement them in your life. Now let's continue to explore a few more strategies that can help boost your creativity enough.

Doubt Every Default or Assumption

Thomas Edison used to offer a bowl of soup to the candidates who would visit him for any job interview.

He had a strange way of testing the candidate's aptitude before shortlisting him for the position. He outrightly rejected those candidates who sprinkled salt in the soup without testing it. Edison believed that anyone who wants to invent things should have the ability to doubt the default. In his view, if someone already assumed that the soup didn't have salt in it, they didn't question or test the assumption before taking further action.

Take another example. There was an assumption in the industrial age that the manual workers need to travel physically to the respective processes used in heavy machinery, and *vice versa* was not possible. But Henry Ford doubted this assumption and the result was the invention of the assembly line in the automobile industry. The item being manufactured would travel to the skilled worker through the assembly line, and that itself revolutionized the productivity and speed of the manufacturing process manifold while saving time, energy, and efforts of the manual workers.

If you want to think out of the box, you need to doubt the assumption.

There could be two types of doubts:

- **Self-Doubt** – It is paralyzing, because you get demoralized and don't take any action. To overcome this, you need to develop your beliefs, as we explained in greater details in our previous chapter about how to build your inner infrastructure.

- **Idea doubt**- In this approach, you make it more interesting, you take this as a challenge and try to find out the real solutions by doubting the validity of the idea.

There was a survey carried out, and it was revealed that the people who installed Firefox or Chrome web-search platform were more creative than the people who just worked with Internet Explorer or Safari application.

Why was it so?

The reason was the people who installed Firefox or Chrome challenged the assumption that the existing applications that came installed with the computer were the best ones. They instead took efforts to install other applications that they perceived to give better experience. This set of people was willing to doubt the default and try something different.

In order to be more creative and generate a new set of ideas:

- You should start doubting any and all kind of default settings as the only way to go for. For example, if someone recommends some product or service, as he or she is using it, then you don't need to immediately accept their default choice, you need to question and explore the other options as well.

- You need to develop the habits of questioning the assumption. The common assumption is that every employee needs to be at work for 8 hours. But have you ever asked why each employee needed to spend the same amount of hours at work? You can question that what if someone finishes their work in 4 hours, then why shouldn't they be allowed to spend their time meeting someone out of office, or attend some event or program or meet new people, that can bring more business to the organization?

Doubting the default is the first step in innovating things. If you are already fine with whatever is there, then you'd never think of ways to improve it. Therefore, you need to start doubting the assumptions more often to trigger a challenge in your mind to do better.

Questions. Questions. Questions = Ideas. Ideas and Ideas

Great innovators always ask questions and a variety of questions every time they encounter some problem or challenge.

It's the quality of question that determines the quality of life. Questions cause you to stretch, grow, and think beyond what's real on the ground and activate your imagination.

Questions bring you out of the certainty of knowledge and lead you to an uncertain world you are not familiar with. Certainty narrows your worldview and uncertainty broadens and deepens your scope. When you know that you are certain, you don't explore much, but when you invite uncertainty in your life, you want to come out with better ideas.

Eugene Ionesco says, "It is not the answer that enlightens, but the question."

Isaac Newton asked, "Why does an apple fall from a tree?" and, "Why does the moon not fall into the Earth?"

Eric Schmidt, Executive Chairman of Google's parent company, Alphabet, once said, "We run this company on questions, not answers."

Here is what Albert Einstein said about curiosity and the power of questions:

"Don't think about why you question, simply don't stop questioning. Don't worry about what you can't answer, and don't try to explain what you can't know. Curiosity is its own reason. Aren't you in awe when you contemplate the mysteries of eternity, of life, of the marvelous structure behind reality?

And this is the miracle of the human mind—to use its constructions, concepts, and formulas as tools to explain what man sees, feels, and touches. Try to comprehend a little more each day. Have holy curiosity."

Gary Keller, author of one of my favorite book, *The One Thing,* talks about The Focusing Question, where he challenges us to ask one specific type of question that will force you to focus on your most important things. The Focusing Question is: *"What is the one thing that I can do, such that by doing that thing, all other things become either very easy or become unnecessary"*

Therefore, to generate a new set of ideas, ask a newer set of questions. Here is what you can do to make questioning a daily habit of your life in all areas by asking some standard questions.

- Why is it that I'm following a particular approach to handling my most important project?

Then answer this question and find a stronger reason that pulls you. If you don't find a stronger reason by asking it numerous times, it's time to change your approach or even the work.

- What else can I do to speed up the execution of my work?

This question will probably prompt you to jump to Google with a question "How to do _____ (type your work here) in half of the time and cost?" Or ask if there is a way to outsource the work that someone else can do at a fraction of the cost of my time.

- Who should I be meeting or consulting that can improve the pace of my growth in my life?

This question should immediately trigger you to pull out your pen and paper and start writing the names of the people you know and you think can help you suggest the better ways of handling the work.

- When is the optimum time to do any particular thing, so that I generate maximum ROTI (return on time invested.)

You'll realize that at certain points in time in your day, you are either more energized to handle difficult work or at some point in time in your work day, it's much calmer and there is less distraction, where you should do your most focused work.

You might feel more energetic early in the morning and motivated enough to crack on your most important task, when others are sleeping at home, or else, you might be a night owl and want to keep pushing late in the night.

- How should I improve the quality of my personal life, relationship with others, and live in a more fulfilled way?

Seeking the answer to this question will trigger your mind to generate different ways to activate these feelings. Maybe you will start looking for some events or conference over the weekend that can enhance your knowledge and understanding and the options available. Maybe you choose to get into some deeper meditation practice to seek answers from within.

Ask questions for all types of interrogative prefixes like:

- Why
- What
- Who
- When
- How
- Where
- Whether
- If

I've listed some sample questions to give you an idea. But what you should do now is to take a pen and paper and list down your most important projects, be it your personal life, work, relationship, family, adventure, spirituality, and ask these questions from yourself.

Keep writing whatever comes to your mind. You'll either find the answers or trigger some more leading questions about further research or meeting some people or doing some experiments.

If you do this sincerely, you'll surely generate tons of ideas, and hopefully, some of them may serve as your breakthrough ideas that can transform the way you work.

But the key is to keep asking yourself questions. Don't accept the status quo or don't let life keep moving as it has been. You can generate different new ideas with the right set of questions.

Talk to Non-Experts For Great Ideas

In 1861, A German scientist and inventor, Philip Reis, had gone way ahead in his research of inventing the ways of transmitting speech by technology. But he stopped at the advice of experts, who told him that there wouldn't be any commercial viability or the need of transmitting speech, as "the telegram was good enough." And just 15 years later, Alexander Graham Bell registered a patent in his own name for inventing the telephone.

Lord Kelvin, president of Royal Society, in 1895 stated: "Heavier-than-air flying machines are impossible."

Charles Carlson invented Xerography in 1938, but no corporation took his idea seriously, as they believed that carbon paper is cheap and plentiful.

What's common in all the above examples from history? All the predictions about the new ideas by the experts almost went burst; rather, those ideas turned out to be a breakthrough success in history.

Arthur C. Clarke, a British science fiction writer, very rightly said:

"If an elderly but distinguished scientist says that something is possible, he is almost certainly right; but if he says that it is impossible, he is very probably wrong."

The key takeaway here is – if you want to generate innovative ideas, don't seek advice from experts.

Experts have a deep perspective of just a limited subject, which is a good thing for gaining knowledge about that subject, but that limits their understanding about other aspects. The more a person is an expert in one area, the more difficult it becomes for them to form a new idea related to their own subject. Based on their years of experience, they form a certain thinking pattern, and it becomes difficult for them to see through beyond that pattern.

On the other hand, the non-experts (about your subject) do not really have an expertise to draw the borders to any idea related to your subject. They will think openly, widely, and probably their questions might sound quite naïve to the experts. They can see your problem from a distance as an observer (which you can't see because you are too closely associated with the problem) and might come out with some suggestions or advice that gives you an entirely different perspective of looking at the things.

Breakthrough ideas come only through the ability to look at your idea from an independent non-expert's point of view.

Here is what you should do to implement this technique:

- Talk to someone who is outside your field and listen to his ideas and thoughts about how to solve your problem. For example, if you want to generate new ideas to improve your marketing and sales, then meet doctors, engineers, or lawyers, or other unrelated industry people, and understand what would be their process, and ask them what they would think as an observer about your process. You'll get to hear some entirely new thoughts or ideas that you wouldn't have ever generated on your own.

- Surround yourself with idea-oriented people who are exploratory in nature.
- Whenever you meet strangers in any setting, show curiosity in what they do and listen deeply about the way they think about their life and work in general. This may generate some new ideas in your mind.

How to use Procrastination to incubate Ideas

It was the most important evening for Martin Luther King in the year 1963, as the next day, he had to deliver his life's biggest speech ever.

He was up till 3 a.m. rewriting, deleting, and improving certain portions of his speech. After that, he was sitting in the audience and still scribbling his speech notes and making some tweaks here and there. Then the time arrived, he was on the stage with his prepared speech notes.

But just a few minutes into the speech, he left his prepared speech aside and then uttered the four most important words that made history – "I have a dream."

These words were not part of his prepared speech. By procrastinating the preparation of his speech till the last hour, he allowed a longer thinking time for his mind to let the ideas develop. That's what procrastination does. It gives you enough time to consider divergent ideas, to think in non-linear ways, and to make unexpected moves.

Here is the key.

Procrastination is a *vice* when it comes to productivity, but it becomes a *virtue* for creativity.

Adam Grant, in his famous TED speech, talks about how procrastinators develop more creative ideas. The research was done on a few people who were asked to develop some new business ideas. Now, they were divided into two groups. One group was asked to immediately get on the job. The other group was asked to play some game for 5 to 10 minutes before they could think of specific ideas. The people in the latter group were found to be 16% more creative.

Why was it so?

There was nothing special about the game they played. The reason for them being more creative was that they were told about working on a problem and then they were allowed to procrastinate working on the problem – in this case, the task was still in the back of their minds, which allows the ideas to incubate in that space.

Philosopher Ludwig Wittgenstein said, "All great ideas come in the bus, bed, and bath." This is also called three B's of creativity. It means the best ideas come when you are not thinking about them.

Why is it so?

The most famous known examples regarding creativity – that's known as Eureka moment relates to Archimedes, the Greek mathematician. He was asked by a king, who was suspecting that a golden crown contained more silver than gold, to device a method whereby one could know the purity of a metal.

Archimedes spent days and nights on this problem, but couldn't find the answer. Then he thought to keep the problem aside and went for a hot bath in the tub. As he was relaxing in the hot bath, he realized that the water overflowed when he put his body in the water- and this created a unique solution for him. He concluded that a pure gold crown would displace a different amount of water than the one made by an alloy. The history records that he was so excited to find this answer that he ran naked out of his bed in the streets shouting "Eureka"! (I've found it!).

Let's look at another interesting story to understand the power of procrastinating.

William Carrier, a twenty-five-year-old Engineer graduate, was sitting at Pittsburgh Railways station on a foggy day in year the 1902. He was working on the problem of regulating temperature humidity in a printing company. After spending intense time in the problem and not being able to find a solution, he thought to give it a break and therefore was waiting at a station to go for a vacation. He was mindlessly gazing at the fog and mist at the railway station, and suddenly sparked the brilliant idea about the problem that he was working so intensely.

The answer to his problem was air-conditioning. He thought to combine the two technologies, namely electricity and refrigeration. His idea was to blow air through electricity through a fine mist generated through refrigeration, and that would act like a condenser drying out the humid air. Since air's moisture varies at different temperatures, – cold air is drier than warm air. He discovered that change in the temperature of the mist would also alter the level of humidity. And that's how the invention of air-conditioning happened.

Carrier didn't burn himself out by consistently immersing under the problem until it was resolved, rather, he chose to procrastinate finding the solution to the problem – this allowed the required incubation period for his ideas.

In all the above examples, the principle of incubation worked. Your subconscious mind is continually processing information when you have already done the hard work of loading your conscious mind with huge pieces of information. It usually involves setting your problem aside for a few hours, days, or weeks and moving on to other projects. That's why it is recommended to work on multiple projects alongside as we discussed in our earlier point on *slow multi-tasking*.

Though you get away from the challenge, but your subconscious mind continues working on the original challenge in the background. The more interested you are in solving a challenge, the more likely it is that your subconscious will generate ideas.

Incubation helps you put the challenge in perspective. When you leave a problem and come back to it again, you will have a fresh perspective of looking at it.

Here is the step by step process for activating incubation

- **Identify** - What are the challenges you want to solve and how would the solution look like?
- **Prepare** - Prepare as thoroughly as you can from all the sources.

- **Instruct** - Instruct your subconscious mind to find the answer.
- **Incubate** - Now, leave the problem aside - don't work on the problem, go and do something else. Maybe take a shower or go on vacations, etc.
- **Eureka**- the moment will jump out of air suddenly, and you will be supplied with the great idea that can transform your life.

What you should do now?

- Whenever you come across a challenge, the first step that is needed is to do enough research about all aspects of the problem. Read enough literature. Google all the information, search videos, blogs, podcasts on the subject. The test that you have done enough research is that your head starts reeling with loads of information. This means that you have loaded the frontal lobe of your brain called prefrontal cortex, which is responsible for learning new information.

- Now, get away from the challenge for a day or two, or engage yourself into some other project. This will trigger the incubation process, as all the research you have done will start getting processed in your head, and you might get a better solution than what you could have got by forcing your head to give you a solution.

- Stay relaxed and wait for your Eureka moment. It will come at a time and places generally when you least expect it to come.

Just Chill Technique

Stars can't be seen in the day, because their faint points of lights are overwhelmed by the light of the sun. So are your creative ideas, as their subtle nudge mostly get lost in the noisy chit-chat of your brain.

Ideas are already there in the air. Your brain is like a radio station, and only when you tune into the right frequency will you be able to catch the respective radio station. In the case of generating ideas, you become the medium through which the problems get solved, and that happens when you are in a relaxed and meditative state.

Often, we have answers to all our questions, but we don't quiet our minds to see the solution bubbling through the surface.

Wayne Silby, who founded Calvert Impact Capital, a 15 billion dollars investment management group, wrote his designation on business cards as Chief Daydreamer. He used to get into his personal routine of taking a bath in a warm water tank for getting inspiration about ideas. He says[1], "I went into the tank during a time when the government was changing money-market deposit regulations, and I needed to think how to compete with the banks. Floating in the tank, I got the idea of joining them instead. We wound up creating an $800 million program. Often, we already have the answers to our problems, but we don't quiet ourselves enough to see the solutions bubbling just below the surface."

While we are awake, our brain works in Beta brainwaves, which is not an ideal condition for ideas to come up. To generate creativity, you need a calmer and relaxed state of mind that comes with Alpha brainwaves.

Let's understand these different types of brainwaves.

Beta brainwaves have a frequency of 12 Hz to 40 Hz, which is a high frequency of waves. The more you work under the influence of these waves, the more you are supposed to get affected by anxiety, stress arousal, inability to relax, etc.

Alpha brainwaves have a frequency range of 8 Hz to 12 Hz, this is a moderate level. If you are under the influence of these brainwaves more, you get in the state of daydreaming, too relaxed, and unable to focus on any one thing.

Here is the road map for getting into Alpha Brainwaves state:

Below are the elements that help you transition into an Alpha state smoothly:

1. **A quiet environment**: you should be in an entirely undistracted and quiet environment.
2. **Use specific mental relaxation technique**: You have to choose any of the relaxing technique that helps you to enter into a deep meditative state. If you already follow some relaxation technique, be it some kind of mindfulness meditation or any other practice, you should get into a relaxed state of mind, as it is a prerequisite to get into Alpha-brainwave state.

There is one more technique that can be used for relaxation, that's called Jell-O-Syndrome, which is a deep-muscle relaxation technique.

Here is how you can do it to relax yourself from head to toe.

Get comfortable. The basic technique is to relax your body by relaxing each muscle in turn, from your toes to your scalp.

Imagine that as each muscle relaxes, the tension flows out of your body. Try to relax each muscle group sequentially without exerting too much conscious effort. Let go a little at a time, stop frowning, let your arms, hands, shoulders, and jaw go.

By systematically relaxing your muscle groups, you can achieve a state of deep relaxation in which the conscious is subdued and quieted, and that still, small voice from the unconscious can come through.

If you have trouble relaxing your muscles in sequence, imagine that your body is a series of inflated rubber balloons. Two valves open in your feet, and your legs begin to collapse until they are two deflated rubber tires lying flat. Next, the valve in your chest is opened, the air escapes, and your entire trunk goes limp. Continue with your arms, neck, and head.

Once your body is totally limp, breathe deeply and slowly from your stomach. Fill your lungs with air. Breathe in slowly and then exhale slowly. Do it until you feel totally free and relaxed.

3. **A passive attitude**: You have to empty your mind. Don't dwell on the thoughts as they pass through your consciousness.

4. **A comfortable position**: Find a comfortable sitting position, in

which you can sit there for at least 15 minutes or so.

You can become the medium through which any problem solves itself by using relaxation and meditation. This technique produces alpha brain waves that are slower and deeper than beta waves. If you can transition yourself in the state of Alpha brainwaves, then you'll start generating and attracting the solutions, as alpha waves quiet your mind so you can see the solutions that are already there.

Chapter 6 Key Takeaways

In this chapter, you learned a few more techniques for creative thinking and generating more ideas:

1. **Doubt the Default- Question the Assumption**: You should never accept the default situation and rather, question it. Only if you challenge the assumption or default situation would you be able to force your mind to think about other alternatives.

2. **The Power of Questions**: The quality of your life depends on the quality of the questions you ask yourself. All great innovators like Albert Einstein, Isaac Newton, Elon Musk have the habit of asking powerful and imaginative questions. Asking questions nourishes your curiosity and forces your mind to generate different ideas. Use What, Why, When, Where, How questions more often in relation to any of your challenge to generate creativity on demand.

3. **Talk to Non-Experts to get creative ideas**. While experts have a deep understanding of one subject, but at the same time, they have very limited knowledge about other broad areas. Arthur C. Clarke, a British writer, puts it in a crux, "If an elderly but distinguished scientist says that something is possible, he is almost certainly right; but if he says that it is impossible, he is very probably wrong." So you should look out for non-expert people's views on things when your objective is to generate innovative ideas.

4. **Procrastination boost Creativity**: While Procrastination is a vice for productivity, it is a virtue for creativity. Procrastination gives the creators enough time to let the different thoughts incubate and germinate new combination of ideas. You can use the 5 step process as a roadmap to activate the incubation of ideas.

5. **Chilling out technique**: This is more of a passive technique to generate innovative ideas. You transition yourself from distractive and noisy beta brainwaves to relaxing Alpha brainwaves. And this lets your mind to get into more of an imaginative and daydreaming state, where you can invite more ideas.

Conclusion

****

"Imagination is more important than knowledge. Knowledge is limited. Imagination encircles the world."

~ *Albert Einstein*

And this brings us to the end of this book.

Now, you are equipped with all the understanding about how out of the box thinking works. You are well aware of many creative thinking techniques that can supply you with more than a handful of ideas to handle your challenges in different areas of your life.

I wrote this book in a manner that you could use and implement the techniques while reading the book. I hope you had taken out time alongside to do the required exercises and if yes, I'm sure you'd have already experienced a rise in your creative thinking abilities.

However, I understand that some people first want to understand the whole concept by reading the complete book before trying to implement that. If you are in that category, no worries, you can now start revisiting the exercises to see the results for you.

Let me be candid. Though I write my books specifically to add value to the lives of my readers (it's you!), but I always have some personal motive in my head to get exposed to valuable insights while doing research so that I can get benefitted by implementing them in my life.

Therefore, I invite you to this journey with me to practice what we just learned in the book and deepen our experience of life by experimenting with multiple creative thinking techniques.

To help you get a quick summary, I've captured all the big ideas of every chapter at the end of the respective chapter so that you can have a bird's eye view of the content.

As we all know, repetition is the mother of learning. So let's keep exposing our minds to the resourceful information on a regular basis, and let the compound effect work to our advantage in developing a creative mind and lead a life of joy, abundance, and success.

I wish you nothing but loads of success by generating and implementing great ideas in all your endeavors.

Cheers

May I ask you for a small favor?

At the outset, I want to give you a big thanks for taking out time to read this book. You could have chosen any other book, but you took mine, and I totally appreciate this.

I hope you got at least a few actionable insights that will have a positive impact on your day to day life.

Can I ask for 30 seconds more of your time?

I'd love if you could leave a review about the book. Reviews may not matter to big-name authors; but they're a tremendous help for authors like me, who don't have much following. They help me to grow my readership by encouraging folks to take a chance on my books.

To put it straight– **reviews are the life blood for any author.**

Please leave your review by clicking below link, it will directly lead you to book review page.

DIRECT REVIEW LINK FOR "THINK OUT OF THE BOX"

It will just take less than a minute of your time, but will tremendously help me to reach out to more people, so please leave your review.

Thanks for your support to my work. And I'd love to see your review.

Full Book Summary

Chapter 1- Introduction: Key Takeaways

Even if you apparently find limited alternatives to any problem, there are still more solutions to any problem; and that's possible with out of the box thinking.

Individuals and organizations equally can challenge their existing way of operations and observe the things by shifting their perspective and approach of looking at any problem. The personal, as well as organization level examples, demonstrate that out of the box thinking opens up new paradigms and widens the perspective of looking at the world.

Also, **out of box thinking is not uniquely gifted to some artistic profile people, nor is it limited to reality-bending world-changing successful entrepreneurs**. Anyone can develop their creative thinking faculties and generate surprisingly new and unpredictable ways of solving problems, if they believe so and are willing to spend time and effort in learning how to do out of the box thinking.

This book is a roadmap to **learning and implementing the strategies for every growth-oriented individuals**, who want to explore and lead their life in a way that they couldn't have comprehended earlier.

Chapter 2: Key Takeaways

Your thinking can be compared to a box. The box has limitation about storing a specific quantity, as well as only specific type of items can be put in a particular box. Similarly, our minds tend to think in a particular way all the time, which is generally limited in nature and controlled by the type of thoughts that are unconsciously fed in our brains since our childhood till we become independent adults. The result is **human mind thinks only in a certain specific conditioned way.**

The 9-dot exercise helps you assess your way of thinking, whether you follow the conventional inside the box approach or go out of the box to solve the problem innovatively. The only way to thinking differently and creatively is to come out of the limited box and experience the limitless options around you, unforeseeable from inside-the-box thinking approach.

Before science could look deeper into the brain i.e., until the middle of the twentieth century, **it was believed that the left brain is the superior portion of our brain**, and the other side i.e., the right brain is a retarded and impractical dreamer stuff, which doesn't serve any utility for the material world outside.

Thanks to the research by Robert Sperry, Nobel Prize winner, where he showed to the world **that the right hemisphere plays a very important role** by giving a bigger context and understanding of the outside world. Later Betty Edwards, through her book "Drawing from the Right Side of The Brain" and neuroscience, through the innovation of fMRI clearly confirmed how both sides of the brain work.

Each of the brain functions discharged different functions- the left brain controls the right side of the body and vice-versa. The left is sequential, the right is simultaneous. The left brain looks at the text, and the right one focuses on the context. The left brain is analytical, while the right brain synthesizes the information.

Chapter 3 Key Takeaways

Everything starts with a belief. Only if you believe in yourself, your ability to do certain things, you'll think, behave, and act accordingly. No Belief- No Action. The formula is to make a loop i.e., Strong belief >> Massive Actions >> Better Results, which lead to >> even stronger beliefs.

The 3 biggest challenges in building a strong belief are Fear, Uncertainty and Doubt (call them FUDs) and while they are in your head, you'll never believe that you can think differently and come out with creative solutions.

You have to **develop two powerful levers of belief**. (1) That you are capable of doing your part of the job; (2) That something inside of you makes you talented or capable as any other person in the world.

Develop powerful beliefs by Using Tick-Tock Technique. For every negative belief- put them in a "tick" column, and counter them with a strong objective argument in the "tock" column.

Use self-affirmations in the form of "commitment" that makes them feel real and help you develop a new belief system.

Surround yourself with people who evoke a sense of faith in you, and minimize spending time with the people are negative in nature.

Always remember more of your past successes than reminiscing about your failures, because where focus goes, there energy flows.

Chapter 4: Key Takeaways

In this chapter, you learned how you could trigger creativity and further make creativity come to you more often through some daily routines.

Giving a specific and meaningful challenge opens up our mind to generate more ideas than to simply sit and wait for ideas, as your mind wants to be sure of the rewards of being creative.

Alongside the specific challenge to generate ideas, **you need to increase your openness to experiences in your life**. The more experiences you take, the more it will boost your brain's neuroplasticity, and that in turn, will offer more creativity to your brain.

Learning **some musical instruments has been proved by science to increase your creative abilities** more. A few routines can be most important to create more ideas on autopilot basis.

Exercise improves BDNF that is important for memory and creativity. Get more BDNF through intense cardio exercises.

Take Showers: **Taking showers has been proved to generate more dopamine**. The higher the dopamine, the more the possibility of getting creative ideas. Therefore, take more showers.

Follow Open Monitoring Mindfulness meditation. This will open your observation skills – i.e., observing your body and organs from inside, observing outside sounds, smells, and also observing your thoughts, feelings, etc. alongside. The more your observe, the more your divergent thinking skills.

Finally, cut off your cable T.V. connection and watch something you find necessary and important for your mind.

Chapter 5 Key Takeaways

In this chapter, we learned about various techniques to think out of the box and generate more creative ideas.

1. **Feed your head** with a variety of information as a base before you can generate ideas. As Gore Vidal puts it, *"The brain that doesn't feed itself eats itself."* Study a variety of literature, read biographies, read books on subjects other than yours to feed your head with enough information to let ideas germinate and flourish in your brain thereafter.

2. **Use Idea Fusion**: There are no new ideas and often, most of the ideas are just a better combination or a useful improvement over the previous inventions. After you have fed your head with tons of ideas, it's the time to put all those ideas together. Mind mapping is a good technique that you can use to make

all your different ideas come out on paper, so you can make better fusion of the ideas.

3. **Slow Multi-tasking improves creativity**. You should not switch between different tasks in your day to day work, but you should get yourself involved and working on different projects simultaneously. This gives some break from one project and gives your mind a thinking space to let better ideas form over time. Also, you get to make some progress on different projects together.

4. **Use SCAMPER Method**. This method equips you with 7 different ways you could ask questions from yourself. SCAMPER is an acronym, and each letter gives you a specific way to ask a question to generate ideas. It means:

S = Substitute something

C =Combine it with something else

A = Adapt something to it

M = Modify or Magnify it

P = Put it to some different use

E = Eliminate something

R = Reverse Engineer it.

5. **Set a Daily quota for generating ideas**: You should fix a daily quota for yourself to generate at least 5 new ideas for your projects or challenges. You have to develop your idea muscle by practicing daily. The more the number of ideas you have, the better the quality of ideas you can select from them.

6. **Use Boredom to Invite Brilliance**: Getting bored means to not get continuously driven by your frequent cravings and getting distracted often. If you are not doing anything, you'll feel bored. But the benefit of getting bored is it activates your default mode network (DMN) i.e., imagination network of your brain.

By always getting engaged in something puts your other network i.e., Active Network, in continuous mode, and not let DMN offer you the required insights generated by imagination. Therefore, make boredom a part of your life.

Chapter 6 Key Takeaways

In this chapter, you learned a few more techniques for creative thinking and generating more ideas:

1. **Doubt the Default- Question the Assumption**: You should never accept the default situation and rather, question it. Only if you challenge the assumption or default situation would you be able to force your mind to think about other alternatives.

2. **The Power of Questions**: The quality of your life depends on the quality of the questions you ask yourself. All great innovators like Albert Einstein, Isaac Newton, Elon Musk have the habit of asking powerful and imaginative questions. Asking questions nourishes your curiosity and forces your mind to generate different ideas. Use What, Why, When, Where, How questions more often in relation to any of your challenge to generate creativity on demand.

3. **Talk to Non-Experts to get creative ideas**. While experts have a deep understanding of one subject,

but at the same time, they have very limited knowledge about other broad areas. Arthur C. Clarke, a British writer, puts it in a crux, "If an elderly but distinguished scientist says that something is possible, he is almost certainly right; but if he says that it is impossible, he is very probably wrong." So you should look out for non-expert people's views on things when your objective is to generate innovative ideas.

4. **Procrastination boost Creativity** : While Procrastination is a vice for productivity, it is a virtue for creativity. Procrastination gives the creators enough time to let the different thoughts incubate and germinate new combination of ideas. You can use the 5 step process as a roadmap to activate the incubation of ideas.

5. **Chilling out technique**: This is more of a passive technique to generate innovative ideas. You transition yourself from distractive and noisy beta brainwaves to relaxing Alpha brainwaves. And this lets your mind to get into more of an

imaginative and daydreaming state, where you can invite more ideas.

Could you please leave a review on the book?

One last time!

I'd love if you could leave a review about the book. Reviews may not matter to big-name authors; but they're a tremendous help for authors like me, who don't have much following. They help me to grow my readership by encouraging folks to take a chance on my books.

To put it straight– **reviews are the life blood for any author.**

Please leave your review by clicking below link, it will directly lead you to book review page.

DIRECT REVIEW LINK FOR "THINK OUT OF THE BOX"

It will just take less than a minute of yours, but will tremendously help me to reach out to more people, so please leave your review.

Thank you for supporting my work and I'd love to see your review on the book.

Preview of the book "Make Smart Choices"

Introduction

****

> "Success emerges from the quality of the decisions we make and the quantity of luck we receive. We can't control luck. But we can control the way we make choices."
>
> — Chip Heath

A group of children are playing near two different railway tracks.

While one track is operational, the other is disused. Only one child is on the disused track, and the rest of the children are playing on the operational track.

A passenger train is approaching fast.

In this situation, assume you are just standing beside the track interchange. You are in control of the track and can change the track whatever way you decide. Since, you are standing quite far from the children, you don't have enough time to go or shout to the kids about a fast approaching train.

You have two choices here.

You can make the train change its course to the disused track and save most of the kids by sacrificing the life of a lone child playing on the disused track. Or would you rather let the train go on its way?

Most people would choose diverting the course of the train and sacrifice only one child to save the lives of ten children.

One life versus ten – ten lives are more precious. Seems an obvious decision, doesn't it?

When I heard this the first time, I instantly thought this way only because saving the lives of many children by sacrificing life of one child appears to be a rational decision that most people would make, morally and emotionally.

But pause for a moment and think a bit harder. What is the fault of the child choosing to play on the disused track, who in fact made a right decision to play in a safe place?

Why does his life warrant a sacrifice merely because his ignorant friends chose to play where the danger was?

Leo Velski Julian, a critic who told the above story, said he would not try to change the course of the train because he believed that the kids playing on the operational track should have known very well that the track was still in use, and they should have run away when they heard the train's siren.

If the train had been diverted, that lone child would definitely die because he never thought the train would come over to that track. Moreover, that track was not in use probably because it was not safe. If the train had been diverted to the track, the lives of all passengers on board would have been at stake. And in your attempt to save a few kids by sacrificing one child, you might end up sacrificing hundreds of people.

You might have realized by now how a decision that immediately seemed like a straight forward choice (though emotionally a bit hard) can prove to be a worse choice, with a little bit of thinking.

Life sometimes offers tough choices in disguised form, and making hasty decisions in such situations may not always be the right move.

Though all the decisions in front of us are not of life or death situations, still there is no denying that we have to make decisions almost all the time.

Every Moment is a Moment of Choice

Every day and every moment, we have to make some kind of decision: they add up. They could be miniature choices with minimal impact, or they could be big decisions that can change the trajectory of your life.

A few examples of simple and low (or no) impact choices could be:

- What to eat, which restaurant to visit, or what cuisine/dish to order?
- What to wear to your office or a party today?
- What route to take to the office if you are late, so you don't get into heavy traffic?
- Which movie to watch this weekend, with whom to go, and what theatre?
- Whether to go out for drinks with friends or have a fun evening with the kids?

You see that the above decisions are really simple decisions, and the difference is just some moments of pleasure if you make them right, or a sad evening, if you don't choose correcting.

But there are times when life requires you to take a leap forward and make huge decisions like:

- What career to opt for or which college/university to enter?
- What companies to apply to for jobs?
- Whether to continue in the same job, change jobs, or make an altogether career move and explore new ways to reach your dreams.
- Should you marry now or wait 3-4 years? What kind of life partner to the tie knot with?

- If you get married, do you want to have kids now or in a few years?

The above questions are difficult, life-altering decisions with high stakes, and the consequences will keep tormenting you for years if you don't make the right choices.

You see, all decisions are not equal, so they don't pose an equal level of challenge. Some decisions take less energy and others take lot of time, effort, and even cause a lot of stress. Any decision becomes easy or difficult depending on the stakes involved. Choosing a food item from a menu is easier than finding employment in a new sector or starting a business venture.

The bottom line is that the nature of problems may vary, but you have to make decisions -- small decisions and big decisions every time.

Therefore, it wouldn't be incorrect to say: You don't have a choice except to make a choice.

You Still Make Decisions Even If You Think You Don't

There's one intriguing approach a few people follow. They think if they don't make any decisions, they will remain safe from the risks involved and the consequences that can arise.

But here is the thing.

Not making a decision is also a choice. Unconsciously, you might think you have not decided, but, in effect, you have chosen to ignore the situation, which in itself is a decision.

If you <u>don't wake up after your alarm goes off</u> and continue to stay in the bed, while you could hit the gym, you have unconsciously decided to choose laziness instead of fitness.

If you are <u>stuck in a job or are inadvertently trapped in a low-rewarding business</u> that no longer fascinates you, and you don't do anything about it, you've made a decision – a decision to let boredom, unhappiness and soon-to-be-highlighted issues of low performance emerge in your life.

If you <u>don't do anything and say you'll see and handle whatever happens in the future</u>, then you are choosing not to improve yourself per the changing demands of the environment, thus inviting in the troubles of becoming obsolete in the marketplace.

Yes, you made decisions in all the above cases, though you might erroneously think you haven't.

Take this famous real-world example of what happened to a huge corporation that chose not to make a decision.

Kodak was a pioneer in film-based photography. The giant was a market leader during times when cameras required inserting physical film to take pictures that later needed to be developed through a chemical process to generate a physical photograph. Unlike today's digital cameras, you had no way of knowing how they would look, until you saw the physically-developed prints.

Kodak continued to produce film-based cameras for decades and was ruling the industry. Despite the fact that digital photography was invented by a Kodak engineer, the management simply ignored it. During the later years of twentieth century, when digital photography was emerging, Kodak didn't pay the required attention to this new disruptive technology and all but missed the digital wave.

What was the result? New digital camera companies started enjoying dominance in the camera business, rising over Kodak, and it was not long before Kodak had to shut down its shops.

What was wrong with Kodak's approach?

Kodak just continued what it had been doing for years. It simply did not decide, and this non-decision proved to be the worst decision of Kodak.

In a nutshell, you have to make decisions every time, and if you don't decide, don't kid yourself, you have still made the decision not to make a decision.

Decision making, therefore, is one of the most important life skills.

What You'll Learn in This Book

My objective in writing this book is to empower you think better and make smarter decisions by developing the right mental framework and applying actionable strategies. This book will make you aware of your decision-making archetype based on the end objective behind any choices. You will learn about four different types of decision makers and what makes them decide so differently.

You'll learn the common struggles that most people face in making decision and come to know about the hidden traps that lead to bad choices. It's only when you become aware of these traps or obstacles that you start making changes in your approach, because awareness is the very first step in any kind of transformation. Until you realize what is bad, you really don't have any motivation to change yourself.

This book is loaded with scientific and psychological research to help you overcome your thinking biases or erroneous beliefs and equip yourself with new tools and parameters to decide more intelligently and make better and more decisions in less time.

--End of Preview--

Get your copy of the full book >>> *Make Smart Choices*

Other Books in <u>Power-Up Your Brain Series</u>

1. ***Intelligent Thinking:*** *Overcome Thinking Errors, Learn Advanced Techniques to Think Intelligently, Make Smarter Choices, and Become the Best Version of Yourself (Power-Up Your Brain Series Book 1)*

2. ***Think Out of The Box:*** *Generate Ideas on Demand, Improve Problem Solving, Make Better Decisions, and Start Thinking Your Way to the Top (Power-Up Your Brain Series Book 2)*

3. ***Make Smart Choices:*** *Learn How to Think Clearly, Beat Information Anxiety, Improve Decision Making Skills, and Solve Problems Faster (Power-Up Your Brain Series Book 3)*

4. ***Build A Happier Brain:*** *The Neuroscience and Psychology of Happiness. Learn Simple Yet Effective Habits for Happiness in Personal,*

Professional Life and Relationships (Power-Up Your Brain Book 4)

5. ***Think With Full Brain:*** *Strengthen Logical Analysis, Invite Breakthrough Ideas, Level-up Interpersonal Intelligence, and Unleash Your Brain's Full Potential (Power-Up Your Brain Series Book 5)*

Copyright © 2019 by Som Bathla

All rights reserved. No part of this book may be reproduced in any form without permission in writing from the author.

No part of this publication may be reproduced or transmitted in any form or by any means, mechanical or electronic, including photocopying or recording, or by any information storage and retrieval system, or transmitted by email or by any other means whatsoever without permission in writing from the author.

---

[1] http://upriser.com/posts/new-mcdonald-s-in-phoenix-run-entirely-by-robots

[2] https://www.researchgate.net/publication/8084569_A_Meta-Analysis_of_Personality_in_Scientific_and_Artistic_Creativity
https://www.gwern.net/docs/psychology/1998-feist.pdf

[3] https://www.ncbi.nlm.nih.gov/pmc/articles/PMC3772595/

[4] https://www.ncbi.nlm.nih.gov/pmc/articles/PMC3772595/

[5] **Stanford study finds walking improves creativity**
http://news.stanford.edu/2014/04/24/walking-vs-sitting-042414/

[6] https://www.ncbi.nlm.nih.gov/pmc/articles/PMC3887545/

[7] https://www.frontiersin.org/articles/10.3389/fpsyg.2012.00116/full

[8] https://www.psychologicalscience.org/news/minds-business/observation-skills-may-be-key-ingredient-to-creativity.html#.WUPjYxPyvdQ

[9] http://contemplative-studies.org/wp/index.php/2015/07/25/beginning-meditation-getting-started-4-open-monitoring-meditation/

[10] https://www.nytimes.com/1993/05/02/magazine/vikram-seth-s-big-book.html

[11] http://www.npr.org/2013/05/10/182861382/the-myth-of-multitasking
[12] https://www.businessinsider.com.au/spanx-ceo-sara-blakely-fake-commute-2018-11
[13] https://www.medicaldaily.com/human-attention-span-shortens-8-seconds-due-digital-technology-3-ways-stay-focused-333474
[14] From Thinkertoys, A handbook to Creative Thinking Techniques by Michael Michalko

Printed in Great Britain
by Amazon